Mystics and the World of Work:

31 Meditations for Modern Managers

George M. Alliger

StJD Press
Houston

StJD Press, Houston

Typeset in Times New Roman

Library of Congress Control Number: 2025902763

ISBN: 979-8-218-60229-1

In Memoriam

Harold Horowitz,

Manager Extraordinaire

1936-2021

Contents

Contents

Contents

Introduction

The why of the book; what the reader can expect

> "I wish I had read more of the mystics earlier in my life." – Albert Einstein
>
> "In the end we are always rewarded for our good will, our patience, fairmindedness, and gentleness with what is strange." – Friedrich Nietzsche

If a manager were to follow Albert Einstein's implicit advice to read and ponder the words of a few mystics – whether Sufi, Buddhist, Hindu, Christian, Jewish, or other – would that be useful in his or her work? Would it uncover guidance on how to support and lead a team or department? Could it increase the clarity of one's role in the workplace?

Because – in the typical way of looking at things – a Venn diagram mapping mystical insights to the psychology of management would simply show non-overlapping circles. Managers are pragmatists, mystics are "out there." There is management science, and there is mysticism. There are managers and supervisors, and there are mystics and contemplatives – but are managers ever mystics? Or mystics, managers?

The single most distinctive feature of this book may be its reconsideration of this apparent mutual exclusion. Other aspects of the book that I hope are useful include a) the range of mystics considered, b) the folding in of the perspectives of clinical, social, and industrial/organizational psychology, and c) the structure of the book as short "meditations for managers."

* * *

Mysticism has a unique way of seeing and valuing the world, including the world of work. It perceives reality in deeper and different terms than does, say, the Harvard Business Review or the Academy of Management. The HBR will of course provide tips, rules, techniques, best practices, and instructions to help you face the challenges of daily management. The AoM can offer results from academic studies designed to ferret out the details and quirks of numerous managerial dynamics – and highlight, for each study, some "practical implications" or take-home lessons. There are many institutions like HBR and AoM, and their messages are disseminated to organizations by various means, including by the many consultants and consulting firms inhabiting the business landscape.

And these HBR- or AoM-type approaches "follow the science;" the guidance they provide is "evidence-based."

Certainly, mystics shouldn't claim to be scientific. And for the most part, they do not so claim. But they do claim to have actual insights into the nature of reality. It may be that mystics, when they speak, are reporting back to us from the rim – the leading edge – of reality. Such reports, apparently, are based on intuition and faith. But they are not therefore necessarily useless or uncertain as guides for our activities. Whether mysticism is "useful" is a pragmatic question.

In fact, pragmatism, for example as formulated by psychologist William James, supports a reexamination of whether mysticism and management are truly non-overlapping. James favored the idea that what is sometimes denied authority as being "unscientific" – for example, religion – validates itself when and wherever it shows practical effects in the lives of people. Management, I believe, is one of the domains where the wisdom of the mystics can be shown to be pragmatic in this sense. And after all, "Science cannot solve the ultimate mystery of nature," said physicist Max Planck. "And that is because, in the last analysis, we ourselves are part of nature and therefore part of the mystery that we are trying to solve." So where science stops providing useful advice, mysticism may start.

It is probably true that the primary motivations of mysticism are not to be pragmatic or useful. But taking its perspective can have these effects. It's easy to see why deep perception into the full nature of the universe, both visible and invisible – and the attendant personal peace – can be useful or applicable to work. Even if such insights and consequences are not sought out *in order* to be applied.

Of course, following good, standard business tips and techniques is likely to be easier than following the mystics. This is because their vision of things may require self-change. Instead of simply acting within the workplace more effectively, you may be asked to work on yourself. Or what is harder, allow yourself to be worked on.

* * *

As mentioned, in addition to the most important characteristic of this book, namely the examination of potential overlaps between the topics of management and mysticism, there are significant others. These include the sweep of mystics whose principles and sayings will be cited. Although many of the mystics cited will be those to whom the term traditionally applies (Islamic Sufis, Zen masters, Hasidic visionaries, Christian mystics, Jewish sages, Hindu gurus), the definition of "mystic" will not be strict. Included will be some philosophers (e.g., Ludwig Wittgenstein, Simone Weil, Alfred North Whitehead), scientists (e.g., physicists Neils Bohr, David Bohm, Erwin Schrödinger), literary figures (e.g., William Blake, Jorge Luis Borges), and psychologists (e.g., Carl Jung, William James), to each of whom can be attributed writings or statements that are clearly mystical.

Also, the research findings and writings of various fields of psychology will both challenge and round out the thoughts of the mystics as they apply to management. Psychological research can help translate for the modern manager what the mystics teach. Other times, psychological research can seem to disagree with the statements of mystics, which is interesting in itself. I find that in these cases, however, there is usually a way to bridge the chasm.

* * *

One strange thing encountered by anyone who considers the utterances of the mystics is the fact that they would often rather not utter anything at all. This is because words don't seem to successfully transmit what they have experienced. You probably have noticed yourself that it can be difficult to explain exactly what it is you are feeling, particularly when you feel overwhelmed or have an acute perception of some, as it seems to you, truth. It isn't that what you feel is unclear, but rather that words – no matter which words, in whatever sequence – seem a rather pitiful reflection of it. As Arthur Koestler put it in his *The Invisible Writing*, "'Mystical' experiences, as we dubiously call them, are not nebulous, vague or maudlin — they only become so when we debase them by verbalisation."

Thus there is, apparently, an extreme mismatch between the specificity and reach of what a mystic perceives and the ability of words to capture those perceptions. As a result, there can be no question that some, perhaps most, mystics remain silent. It is impossible to know how many of these there are among us – they simply cannot be detected. As Lao Tsu stated, "those who know do not speak."

Luckily for us, Lao Tsu himself didn't hold fast to this dictum. He did speak, as did a sizeable subset of mystics.

That speech, however, often seems difficult to understand. Metaphors, similes, and apparent paradoxes populate the landscape of mystical writings. Statements can seem outrageous or simply opaque. They are unlike a straightforward equivalence (2 + 2 = 4), description (this dish is white), or command (go to the door). Rather, a mystical formulation is, as the Zen saying has it, "a finger pointing to the moon." The finger is not the thing to be focused on – although it tries to indicate what one *should* focus on.

Hence the concept of meditating upon sayings. Their meaning(s) may only become clearer as you let them sit in your thoughts for a while. Even then you may feel you are seeing as through a mist. "Now we see only a dim likeness of things," St. Paul says. "It is as if we were seeing them in a foggy mirror." Glimpses of clarity can occur then vanish. An "ah ha!" may need to be recaptured again and again.

But ignoring the mystics because they seem obscure is to leave unopened a treasury of insight. And this treasury is, in fact, probably more often left unopened than otherwise. Ludwig Wittgenstein noted that, alas, "a key can lie forever in the place where the locksmith left it, and never be used to open the lock the master forged it for."

* * *

This book is not really just for managers. It is for employees too, and anyone interested in the topic. Many of the insights that we can perceive in the mystics apply to any and all facets of life, strange though those insights may seem at first blush. Given that strangeness, the quote from philosopher Friedrich Nietzsche at the head of this introduction is worth pondering: "In the end we are always rewarded for our good will, our patience, fair-mindedness, and gentleness with what is strange."

Each meditation or reflection in this book stands alone, addressing some angle of management. The reader can therefore read, and ponder, them in any order.

Koestler, A. (2005). *The invisible writing.* Random House.

New International Reader's Version Bible. (1979). Grand Rapids, Zondervan.

Nietzsche, F. (2010). *The Gay Science: With a Prelude in Rhymes and an Appendix of Songs.* Vintage.

Planck, M. (2017). *Where is science going?* Pickle Partners Publishing.

1. Can You Be in Two (or More) Places at Once?

Mystical bilocation and being present to remote workers

When Greek mathematician and philosopher Pythagoras wanted to meet with friends, even if they were in a different country, he would simply appear to them, and they would converse.

I spent my junior year of college at Banaras Hindu University. This is in Varanasi, India, and is truly huge, with over 18,000 residential students. I reveled in its classic Indo-Gothic architecture, was challenged by the heat of the campus cuisine, and of course took various courses. But I also carried out a personal, informal study of *gurus* and *sannyasa*. Varanasi (previously Banaras) is perfect for such an exploration, being the holiest city in India; pilgrims can wash away their sins in the Ganges River, which flows through the city. Hence, holy people of different persuasions are many and conspicuous, and it is easy to strike up conversations.

Gurus, as you likely know, are Hindu religious teachers; they usually have disciples ("*chelas*"). A *sannyasi* (or *sannyasini* if female), by contrast, is simply a Hindu who has entered the fourth stage of life. This involves the renunciation of material desires. They may travel about the country. (The other three, earlier, stages are *brahmacharya* or student, *grihastha* or householder, and *vanaprastha* or retired, pre-*sannyasa*).

One day while roaming about the city, I encountered a *guru*. From the beginning of our conversation, he was interested in telling me about his powers. One intriguing claim he made was this: "I have many followers. Some live near here, others in villages farther away. They have told me that I visit them. They see me, though I have not moved from my abode."

This ability to be in two places at once struck me as odd and rather unbelievable.

Not all encounters with guru-like people were like that. For example, initially I believed that all the wandering *sannyasa* that I saw on the streets were renunciates, having given up possession of material goods. I recall one, robe-clad, dignified and tall, with staff in hand. I said something about how hard it must be to manage day to day, having renounced money. He quickly punctured the whole premise. "Oh," he said, "I have a lot of money in various places – not just cash but securities and stocks." So renunciation of the material world, apparently, can be accomplished in a purely inner way.

However, let's revert to the guru who claimed to be able to appear to distant followers without traveling. This miraculous ability is known, sensibly enough, as "bilocation." And, as you might suspect, reports of bilocation are rare. But not vanishingly so. Consider Greek philosopher Pythagoras (c. 570 – 495 BCE). We know little for sure about his life, but he is famous for a variety of accomplishments. These include the famous theorem for determining the hypotenuse of a triangle which you learned about in school, and for arguments in support of reincarnation, which you probably did not learn about. In any case, the philosopher Porphyry said that it was generally agreed that Pythagoras could bilocate. He did this to converse simultaneously with friends in different countries, even though "the places are separated by many miles, both at sea and land, demanding many days' journey."

Peruvian St. Martin de Porres (1579 - 1639) appears to have been son of a Spanish gentleman and a previously enslaved woman. Largely ostracized because of his birth, he was nonetheless eventually accepted as a lay brother in Dominican monastery. His remarkable story includes a profound willingness to sacrifice food and comfort for the ill and poor. He was also reported to have the ability to appear in the city at the side of a dying person, providing death bed consolation. He did this, never having left his monastery. Peruvians traveling abroad also would receive helpful visits from him, though he remained at home. Bilocation has been reported for other Catholic saints.

Buddhism too considers this phenomenon entirely feasible, if not commonly displayed. One of the supernormal powers attained by a Buddha is that of producing a different body via the mind, a body having form and "complete with all its limbs and faculties."

With the advent of remote and hybrid work, managers are having to adapt to many meetings that are not face-to-face. However, some studies have shown that virtual meetings can leave workers unusually drained ("Zoom fatigue"). Betty Johnson and Beth Mabry, for example, found that remote meeting load, perception that there are more such meetings than needed to do the job, and the felt need to engage in "surface acting" all contributed to employee emotional exhaustion. This latter variable, surface acting, is a kind of emotional labor, where meeting participants feel it necessary to appear attentive, show positive emotions, or suppress negative ones. And Nan Zhao and colleagues recently used eye-tracking and electroencephalographic technology to compare live versus zoom-like meeting conditions. They found "longer visual dwell times on the real face and also increased arousal as indicated by pupil diameters for the real face condition." Socially relevant systems in the brain were also more activated in the live condition.

These findings reinforce the idea that remote meetings are simply not the same as those held in person. The presumed negative effects are one reason for the fraught conversation now being conducted throughout the business world on return-to-office policies.

Legends of bilocation evoke the power of actual human presence rather than some reduced level of communication, whether writing, auditory, or visual. Few managers will actually be able to bilocate and appear in living and breathing form to a remote employee. In fact, doing so might actually be taken amiss: "How did YOU get in!?"

However, have you mastered a kind of bilocation (or "multilocation") when using Zoom or Teams to conduct a meeting? That is, do you manage somehow to appear "in person," engaging remote employees despite the limitations of the medium? This is surely more art than science. Speaking clearly, listening carefully and looking into the camera are good practices. And keeping these events infrequent, focused and short will help people feel less drained and more appreciative of your "presence."

Pythagoras of Samos (c. 570 – 495 BCE) was a mathematician and may have been the first to call himself a philosopher (lover of wisdom). His broad ranging teachings included not only reincarnation but that the Earth is a sphere with multiple climate zones.

Guiley, R. (2001). *The encyclopedia of saints*. Infobase Publishing.

Johnson, B. J., & Mabry, J. B. (2022). Remote work video meetings: Workers' emotional exhaustion and practices for greater well-being. *German Journal of Human Resource Management, 36(3)*, 380-408.

McMahan, D. L. (2012). *Buddhism in the modern world*. Routledge.

Zhao, N., Zhang, X., Noah, J. A., Tiede, M., & Hirsch, J. (2023). Separable processes for live "in-person" and live "zoom-like" faces. *Imaging Neuroscience, 1*, 1-17.

2. We Ourselves Need to Change First

What if we are our own most limiting factor?

> "We cannot under any circumstances manufacture something which is better than ourselves." – Simone Weil

Should you dip into videos or writings on the topic of Organizational Change, you will be inundated with advice on how best to handle any initiative. To *prepare* for an initiative, you should: Make sure messaging to all employees is clear and buy-in obtained. Identify current and potential objections and obstacles and prepare responses to these. Note where the resisting employees, functions, or departments are and spend especial attention on them. When *launching* the change effort, again pay great attention to messaging and gather information on any problems in the roll out. Pay attention again while the change *works into the ethos and systems* of the company. Then, naturally, *measure* the success of the change. Are all objectives met? If not, why not? What actions can be taken to remediate or fix?

This, of course, is a very abbreviated roadmap for an organizational change. Much more detailed advice is readily available. And a change initiative can be effective if a roadmap is carefully drawn up and executed, with full and enduring support from the leaders of the organization (including managers of all levels).

Such guidance for organizational change is, in a sense, technocratic. That is, it is based on organizational and psychological principles and models. These principles and models are developed first by theory informed by experience, and then honed by both research and further experience.

This short book does not address organizational change, at least not directly.

But the change we focus on here is not organizational, but personal. "Ah," you think, "this is a self-help book then." But I would say not really. Self-help advice is a set of principles or techniques which can be applied to oneself. Pim Cuijpers and Josien Schuurmans helpfully define self-help: "A self-help intervention can be defined as a psychological treatment in which the patient takes home a standardized psychological treatment protocol and works through it more or less independently."

Many of the best self-help techniques are cognitive-behavioral in nature. For example, if the target is your own excessive anxiety, the approaches may involve cognitive "restructuring," systematic relaxation, graded exposure to anxiety-provoking stimuli, and so forth. These have been shown to successfully reduce anxiety in some cases. But they are still techniques.

Mystics recognize that most of us need change. And they offer encouragement and guidance on how that might occur. But – as opposed to organizational researchers and psychologists – mystics tend not to present straight-forward techniques or methods as the way. This is one of the challenges in listening to them and understanding what they really mean.

For mystics favor paradoxes and parables, metaphors and mysteries. Not so much a series of procedural steps, bullet points, or models with boxes and arrows. This is because what a mystic wants to say is not really something that can be said.

It isn't that words or even box-and-arrow models are without meaning. But, says Chuang Tzu, "Meaning has something it is pursuing, but the thing that it is pursuing cannot be put into words and handed down."

Actually, we know this even if we aren't mystics. Let's say someone is training you how to handle difficult conversations with employees. You may learn some methods, some things to do or say, but it is only after repeated experiences of conversing with employees yourself that you see the truth of what you were taught. This happens over and over again: somebody explains something to us, but only experience shows us what is really the case.

Oddly enough, then, words and concrete models cannot really tell us what is really the case. That is what mystics affirm: explicit language cannot capture the meaning that they themselves see. Hence the stories, tales, parables, and paradoxes. These are hints or signs, but they are not certain or clear in some mathematical sense.

In some way, we need to change ourselves if we wish to pierce the insights of the mystics. But this can't happen by simply following clear directions. Unlike for organizational change, for personal change those clear directions don't exist. Or if they do exist, they are so utterly simple and profound that it is impossible to really understand them without already being deeply changed.

But such personal change is important. Simone Weil stated this in a startling way: "We cannot under any circumstances manufacture something which is better than ourselves." This means: we are our own limiting factor. We can try to be the best managers possible, but we ourselves will inevitably create a ceiling for the outcomes of our own efforts. Thus we need to be better to accomplish something better. The focus is on the interior.

Again, though, how is "being better" to be accomplished? Or how are we to probe the enigmatic sayings of the mystics without being mystical ourselves?

The full quotation from Simone Weil offers some insight:

> We cannot under any circumstances manufacture something which is better than ourselves. Thus effort truly stretched towards goodness cannot reach its goal; it is after long, fruitless effort which ends in despair, when we no longer expect anything, that, from outside ourselves, the gift comes as a marvelous surprise.

Here we see that, in fact, we can't change ourselves. We need to be changed, indeed, but (when it comes to seeing what the mystics see) this can only happen as a "gift." It comes from outside us, strangely enough.

Clearly some self-help is efficacious. We should pursue it. But it seems that it will only take us so far. To go further we need to look into the metaphors and paradoxes of the mystics. With the curious proviso that our efforts will be fruitless; our efforts fruitless but in the end – and hopefully along the way! – there will be gifts. These we just need to receive and protect.

Simone Weil (1909-1943) was a French mystic, philosopher, and contradiction. Born into a Jewish family, she professed a kind of unorthodox but profound Christianity. Her most famous book is probably *The Need for Roots*.

Chuang Tzu. (1968). *The Complete Works*. Translated by Burton Watson. Columbia University Press.

Cuijpers, P., & Schuurmans, J. (2007). Self-help interventions for anxiety disorders: an overview. *Current Psychiatry Reports*, *9*, 284-290.

Weil, S. (1997). *Gravity and Grace*. U of Nebraska Press.

Weil, S., & Eliot, T. S. (2003). *The need for roots: Prelude to a declaration of duties towards mankind*. Routledge.

3. People (Including Employees and Managers) are More Like Music Than Machinery

Mechanistic, mathematical, and digital models of employees threaten to create a workplace where people are not understood for what they are

Nothing is more surely and exactly characteristic of modern times than the irresistible invasion of the human world by technology. Mechanism [is] invading like a tide all the places of the earth. – Teilhard de Chardin

If what Teilhard de Chardin saw – the "invasion" of technologies into the world – was like a tide, it has now become a tidal wave. For Teilhard, paleontologist and mystic, was born in 1881. Since then, technologies of all sorts have multiplied until they cling to our lives like barnacles on a ship. Phones, computers, the internet, medical devices, TVs, AI. They are so integrated into our lives that we seem to feel actual pain when parted from them – witness the agonies of both students and parents when a school tries to implement a phone-free environment.

Still, it is quite true that there are many who have been healed or rescued by technological advances such as those in medicine. And, as Steven Pinker carefully documents, much of humanity around the world, due in part to technology, is much healthier and longer-lived than in the century of Teilhard's birth.

But there have been many casualties of technology also. These include our own intimate understanding and sense of ourselves as humans. Specifically, our grasp of ourselves has been undermined by powerful models or metaphors – available in books, movies, and virtually all media – of human beings as motors, machines, and computers.

There is an age-old tendency to use what we construct to image our own construction, to imagine that we are built along the lines of what we can build. We retrieve memories from our "memory bank," we have social "networks," if tired we are "running on empty." And machines and motors are ultimately understandable. In the same way you can troubleshoot a faulty machine, people can in a sense be taken apart, we think, and put back together – perhaps via psychoanalysis.

This is reductionism and scientism. It is not science, which at its best fully grasps that there are limits to its reach. Rather the use of these deterministic models, when taken too seriously, is an invalid extension of science. It is a flight into a clarity that is unwarranted. Humans are not, in fact, particularly easy to understand. We are not particularly reducible to actuators and hydraulics, to rules and algorithms.

When simple mechanisms came on the scene, many philosophers imagined that's what animals and humans were: levers and pulleys. When motors were developed, the human body was understood as a motor. Computers trumped these earlier technologies in creating the conquering metaphor of the human mind as a sophisticated computer. (Sophisticated but not unsurpassable – as many proponents and adversaries of AI argue).

Media and communications professor David Jay Bolter put it this way: "By making a machine think as a man, man re-creates himself, defines himself as a machine." Humans recreate themselves, seemingly willingly, as something less than human.

This is a problem for organizations. They are influenced by this *Zeitgeist*. As neuroscientist and philosopher Iain McGilchrist says, there is "a general trend, throughout the last hundred years or so, towards the ever-greater repudiation of our embodied being, in favour of an abstracted, cerebralised, machine-like version of ourselves that has taken hold on popular thinking." And, if we see ourselves and others as something other, and less than, we truly are, why wouldn't this impact – among other things – how managers manage? Presumably objectifying others, using them as tools rather than negotiating with them as people, is likely if we see the workplace and all its entities and relationships as reducible to mechanisms. In turn, employees themselves will necessarily begin to perceive and even accept a very utilitarian take on things – that everyone in the end is a machine, motor, computer.

A possible reason for the popularity and staying power of these limiting metaphors is that they offer a false precision: they suggest that we understand, or are on the verge of understanding, human nature. Research psychologists have certainly been attracted to such metaphors. Cognitive psychologists, for example, talk of human thinking in terms of input, storage, retrieval, output, and programs. And it is true that they discover some regularities (particularly in sensory systems). But the ability of psychology to generate a full, clear picture of human complexity is quite limited.

This makes sense, since neither human nature, nor the universe, are fully clear. "There is nothing worse," wrote Ansel Adams, "than a brilliant image of a fuzzy concept." Humans, I would argue, are the essence of a fuzzy concept. You *can* make a simple, clear model of the human. It would just be wrong.

Mechanisms such as a fishing rod and reel can be completely understood. They are designed and built to certain specifications. They can be taken apart and reassembled. If they don't work you can figure out why.

Motors and computers are the same; they are, in fact, types of mechanisms – even if computers are digital as well as mechanical. Again, they can be fully understood. Even AI, in theory, is understandable (though its internal associations and weights are too many to waste time on trying to specify).

But even the most ordinary, not to mention the most profound, human experiences can never be reduced to words. This is why music seems to get closer to some truths than do words. Words are limiting; this is the reason Ludwig Wittgenstein spent his life trying to point out, with language, the limits of language.

So perhaps a better figure or representation of the human, rather than a mechanism, motor, or computer, might be something like music.

Music can be talked about, but not understood through talking about it. Consider a professor of music lecturing on a symphony or a popular song. She can say what she likes, but until you hear the composition you really have no idea what he is talking about. And, if you talk about music you have a fair chance of shrinking it, in a way. Music speaks, but not with words. "Compared with music all communication by words," said Nietzsche, "is shameless; words dilute and brutalise; words depersonalise; words make the uncommon common."

Of course, not just music but all of reality eludes words. Music is a good image of this, but it applies to all of experience.

Employees, like all people, cannot be fully analyzed, measured, or even understood. They are in that way like music: you can hear and appreciate them, but as soon as you talk about – or attempt to measure! –them you artificially limit them.

The images of people as machines or computers simply reinforce our tendency to see them as less than they are. And, as managers we may be loath to give up such images, for they suggest that there are ways to control, reinforce, and guide employees using specified techniques, rules, or rewards.

We are awash in real machines and computers. We are (we think, at least) in charge of them. But it's probably better to admit a certain lack of control over employees rather than believe and act as if we are in charge of a bunch of human machines. For, as Pope Francis said, "It is we, and not the machines, who are the true value of work."

Teilhard de Chardin (1881-1955) was a paleontologist, philosopher, and mystic. He was a stretcher-bearer in WWI, a Jesuit priest, and author. His *The Divine Milieu* is a recognized mystical classic, though it – like all his works – was not published during his lifetime.

Bolter, J. D. (1984). *Turing's man: Western culture in the computer age.* UNC Press Books.

https://www.brainyquote.com/quotes/pierre_teilhard_de_chardi_752971

https://www.catholicnewsagency.com/news/255216/pope-francis-people-not-machines-are-the-value-of-work

Koestler, A. (2005). *The invisible writing.* Random House.

McGilchrist, I. (2019). *The master and his emissary: The divided brain and the making of the western world.* Yale University Press.

Nietzsche, F. (1968). *The will to power.* Vintage.

4. Decision Making: A Cat and a Baby

Zen Master Nansen and King Solomon both made a point about decision-making

Once the monks of the Western and Eastern Halls were arguing about a cat. Nansen, holding up the cat, said, "You monks! If you can say a word of Zen, I will spare the cat. Otherwise I will kill it." No one could answer, so Nansen cut the cat in two.

There are lots of great features in this story about Nansen and the cat. I like how mysterious it is. Why were the monks arguing about a cat? Did Zen Masters like Nansen typically have swords and go about cutting things in two? What did he want the monks to say? And if Nansen had a point to make, did he need to kill a cat to do it?

It might not surprise you that some Buddhist authorities doubt the truth of this tale, no doubt in part because of the existence of that religion's prohibitions on killing. Nonetheless, the story comprises one of the *koans*, or puzzles, given for meditation.

For our purposes, maybe we can abstract from the *koan* something to chew on (not the cat itself – neither Buddhists nor anybody else I know eats cat).

There seems to be a simple dynamism underlying the external elements (arguments, cat, sword) of the story. Specifically, Nansen sees in the monks' dispute an opportunity to create a problem or challenge. He does so and demands an immediate solution. They fail to respond, so he himself instantly "solves" the problem he created. Nansen demands a quick decision, and not getting it, makes a quick decision himself.

One key aspect in any manager's work life is that of making decisions. Management researcher and author Henry Mintzberg, in fact, argued that there are three key management roles; decision making is one, the others are interpersonal and informational. *Decisional roles* include Entrepreneur, Disturbance Handler, Resource Allocator, and Negotiator. The *Interpersonal roles* are Figurehead, Leader, and Liaison; these flow from a manager's formal authority and status. *Informational roles* include that of Monitor, Disseminator, and Spokesperson.

Obviously, not all decisions demand a response as immediate as Nansen's. Sometimes it makes good sense to gather information and input from others, understand alternatives, and carefully weigh risk and value. The decisional role of Resource Allocator often will require this kind of thorough thought and investigation, which usually takes some time. But even in resource allocation good management can be demonstrated by firmness and lack of hesitation. In the recent movie *Oppenheimer*, director Christopher Nolan portrays the surprisingly powerful management skills of theoretical physicist J. Robert Oppenheimer. He does this in part by showing actor Cillian Murphy (Oppenheimer) making confident and seemingly instantaneous assignments of people to responsibilities within the atomic bomb project at Los Alamos. The effect in the movie is that the decisions of Oppenheimer both highlight and respond to the urgency of the situation, rather like Nansen with the monks and the cat.

Too, one can see how helpful for all concerned it might be to carry out quick, self-assured decisions in the roles of Disturbance Handler, Negotiator and Entrepreneur.

Where does decision-making ability come from? It seems to be partly due to personality characteristics, but these the relationships to personality are not particularly strong. In any case, personality tends to be stable and resistant to change, although with care and effort one might become more conscientious (for example). But maybe a more fruitful path than trying to change personality is to consider what Nobel prize winner and social scientist Herbert Simon found when he studied how experts make quick decisions.

Specifically, Simon looked at the role of intuition in the making of rapid managerial decisions. What is called intuition allows for such quick decisions by experienced managers. An important word here is "experienced," for it turns out that managers are not immediately intuitive. In the beginning they are deliberate and analytical. But over time people in the managerial role develop an understanding of the *patterns* represented by different situations. Analysis turns slowly to intuition. Eventually, patterns are quickly discerned. This means managers can swiftly respond to situations that on the surface may seem unrelated. As Simon put it, good judgements are "simply analyses frozen into habit and into the capacity for rapid response through recognition."

Maybe there is good news here – intuition grows with experience. Even if part of Oppenheimer's incisive decision-making stemmed from an extraordinary intelligence missing from the rest of us, it was also built on managing students in his teaching roles at various universities, as well as becoming acquainted with the personalities of many leading physicists. And Nansen, too, was presumably an experienced Master by the time of the cat incident.

Intuition, then, can be developed. Analysis becomes automated as it were. This in turn can lead to a kind of relaxed and confident decision making, as situations are quickly recognized and understood. Of course, it is possible to be too confident in one's decisions. As researchers Nathanael Fast and colleagues showed, this seems to be particularly true when a manager both has objective power (is in a position to wield authority) and feels this power subjectively (is aware of that ability to wield power). So humility, as always, is an essential managerial companion.

Humility, and maybe a little inspiration. The episode of Nansen and the cat may have reminded you of a legend about King Solomon. Solomon, of course, was the Israelite king who early on asked God for the gift of wisdom in preference to the gifts of wealth and power. Pleased, God gave him wealth and power as well as wisdom.

This wisdom sparkles in a tale of King Solomon and a baby. Where the monks were fighting over the cat – perhaps each claiming ownership, Solomon was confronted by two women, fighting over the ownership of an infant. Both maintained they were the child's mother. The king proposed to solve the situation by having the baby sliced in two so that each of the claimants could be part owner. Of course, the false mother revealed herself by accepting that solution. And the baby remained whole – perhaps just like Nansen's cat.

Nansen Fugan (c. 749 – c. 835) was a Chinese Zen master during the Tang dynasty. He had his head shaved – began studying Buddhism – at age nine. As an adult, he lived for many years a hermetic life on Mount Nansen (hence his own name). Later he led a monastery where the story of the cat took place.

Fast, N. J., Sivanathan, N., Mayer, N. D., & Galinsky, A. D. (2012). Power and overconfident decision-making. *Organizational Behavior and Human Decision Processes, 117*(2), 249-260.

Mintzberg, H. (1989). *Mintzberg on management: Inside our strange world of organizations.* Simon and Schuster.

Senzaki, N. (2012). *The Gateless Gate* (Annotated Edition). Jazzybee Verlag.

Simon, H. A. (1987). Making management decisions: The role of intuition and emotion. *Academy of Management Perspectives, 1*(1), 57-64.

5. Not Techniques but Being

You cannot impression-manage your way to successful management

> "May your money be destroyed with you for thinking God's gift can be bought!" – St. Peter

These words of St. Peter's are recorded in the book of Acts; he is speaking to Simon, a reputed sorcerer. Simon is reported watching in astonishment as the Apostles Peter and John anoint baptized believers with the Holy Spirit through the imposition of hands. Wanting to add to himself this power, he offers the Apostles money if they will grant it to him. The sorcerer, though, backpedals furiously when Peter points out that the truth cannot be bought, and suggests that both Simon and his bribe should be destroyed.

The small point I'd like to derive from this large story is that, in general, there is no shortcut to authenticity, and that the likeness of a skill is not the authentic skill. More specifically, simulating a thing, however well, is not the thing.

Let's turn to a (somewhat) more worldly example. There is a short, famous book entitled *Zen in the Art of Archery*. In this book Eugen Herrigel tells of his stay in 1920's Japan. There he was an assiduous student of Awa Kenzô, an archery master.

In training Herrigel, Kenzô insisted that his student was not to focus on the details of drawing the bow and shooting targets with arrows. Rather, he was to learn a frame of mind characterized by heightened mental tension and awareness, one in which the arrow would, in effect, eventually release itself. Herrigel, over a long period of time, tried in vain to accomplish this attitude.

Frustrated, he eventually hit upon a technique that simulated this waiting and sudden release. It rather *looked* like the event the master was saying would occur and that he himself had repeatedly demonstrated to Herrigel. Herrigel says,

> I comforted myself with the hope that this technical solution would gradually become so habitual that it would require no further notice from me, and that the day would come when, thanks to it, I would be in a position to loose the shot, self-obliviously and unconsciously, at the moment of highest tension, and that in this case the technical ability would spiritualize itself.

But the simulation of Zen archery did not fool Awa Kenzô, who was instead deeply offended. He immediately threatened, not to destroy Herrigel and his "bribe" – the imitation of the true thing – but to drop him as a student.

The story has a happy ending. Finally – after years of practice and to his own surprise – Herrigel fell into the proper untrammeled state of mind, of being, and could shoot to the master's satisfaction.

Technique and mystery are opposed. Advocates of technique assume that there is no mystery, or if there is, that reality – being in itself – can be successfully fooled by a simulacrum of it. Herrigel tried to fool both himself and the master, but the master was having none of it.

Unfortunately, there are voices in the business world that propose technique over being. Consider "impression management," where a manager (or employee) tries to control what others think about them. One can try to manage impressions via such tactics or techniques such as flattery, ingratiation, self-promotion, justifications, apologies, and the projection of attitudes such as apparent cheerfulness or attentiveness.

Naturally enough, researchers have found that impression management "works" – you can make yourself more liked by others by attempting to appear likable. Many are fooled. But there will be some "masters" in the workforce who will detect it for what it is.

What is a bit disturbing about research in this area is that impression management is usually seen as natural and even inevitable. So, for example, Mark Bolino and colleagues (to pick just a single study) study this topic, and find that employees manage impressions more easily in the beginning just after hire, than later, when more or less stable perceptions have settled in. Therefore "supervisors should consider the initial influence that IM has on their ability to objectively evaluate their new subordinates." That is, they should try to see through or somehow discount attempts at impression management by employees new to their supervision. This is not bad advice, but it never questions whether managing impressions ought to be occurring in the first place.

To some extent, it is certainly true impression management is a natural human reaction to social situations. As I see it, the real problem occurs when it is very consciously adopted as a tactic by either employees or managers. If someone only looks busy, is that the same as being productive? Clearly not. Or, suppose someone seems to approve of an idea you have. Does it matter whether that approval is real or feigned? I would say yes, since honest approval may provide you with actionable information, while false approval means nothing or might even be misleading.

It is the belief that *technique* can somehow achieve *being* that is the most pernicious part of all this. It is not that it is not effective in the moment – it may be. But it can threaten how we understand our lives, which are at root mysterious. As sociologist Jacques Ellul pointed out,

> Far from being restrained by any scruples before the sacred, technique constantly assails it. Everything which is not yet technique becomes so. It is driven onward by itself, by its

character of self-augmentation. Technique denies mystery a priori. The mysterious is merely that which has not yet been technicized.

Technique, then, whether an attempt to simulate a being-based archery, or an attempt to seem to our employees what we are not, can reduce us. In a real way, we are not taking ourselves as seriously as we ought – we are not trusting ourselves – if we adopt techniques to create impressions in others.

St. Peter (d. circa 64 CE). One of the original twelve disciples and considered the founder of the Church in Rome.

Eugen Herrigel (1884-1955) was a professor of philosophy at Tohoku Imperial University in Sendai, Japan in the late 1920s.

Ellul, J. (2021). *The technological society*. Vintage.

Herrigel, Eugen (1989). *Zen in the Art of Archery*. Vintage Books.

New Living Translation. Acts 8:20.

6. Humility

The words of Sufi Ibn Ata Allah al-Iskandari are uncomfortable in any context, including management; but they are worth pondering

> Sufi teacher Ibn Ata Allah al-Iskandari wrote: "Bury your existence in the ground of insignificance because what sprouts out of an unburied seed will not yield good results."

Somewhere I've read that all the virtues will be found in hell, except for humility. And all the sins will be represented in heaven, except arrogance. That is, arrogance can keep you from heaven, and humility from hell. This accords with the blind poet John Milton's take on why Satan himself is in hell – in his pride he sees in himself a greatness that rivals all greatness – including God's. It's "better to reign in hell," says Satan, "than serve in heaven."

However, recent scholarship in *servant leadership* strongly refutes Satan's statement. For many managers, at least, there is an alternative to hungrily seeking and exploiting power. Managing and leading people can be done (and done very effectively) with humility – as someone who uses their power to serve those above, below, and around them.

Servant leadership comprises a cluster of facets or dimensions; there are many different takes on just how many. But, for example, researchers Rakesh Mittal and Peter Dorfman posit and study the nature and effects of five facets; Humility is one. The others are Empathy, Egalitarianism, Moral Integrity, and Empowering and Developing Others. Managers who exhibit these facets in the workplace may expect outcomes such as: greater employee job and task performance, engagement, job satisfaction, and creativity, along with reduced turnover intentions.

Managers, then, who lead with humility can be successful in ways that any organization will prize. This may seem almost counterintuitive, considering our society's seeming preoccupation with leaders as dominant figures.

How can you know if you are managing with humility? Mittal and Dorfman's work suggest that these questions might be helpful: Are you self-effacing, presenting yourself in a modest way? Are you sensitive, aware of even slight changes in others' moods and, when necessary, restricting discussion to prevent embarrassment? Are you modest, presenting yourself without boasting? And are you self-sacrificial, foregoing self-interests and making personal sacrifices in the interest of a goal or vision?

Having these attitudes and displaying these behaviors would indicate managing, in a sense, as a servant. Or consider what the initiator of modern psychological research on this topic, Robert Greenleaf, said was a simple test for whether someone is truly being a servant leader. "Do those served… become healthier, wiser, freer, more autonomous, more likely themselves to become servants?"

Servant management (as we can call it) sounds and presumably is difficult. And it can seem undesirable. Seemingly everyone, including managers, wants recognition. Servant management seems to require a complete lack of calling attention to oneself, a refusal to blow one's own horn. Who wants, as counseled by Ibn Ata Allah al-Iskandari, to bury their existence in the "ground of insignificance?"

Few people *want* to be insignificant, unless it is from fear of some consequences of being known. Sometimes a desire for safety will lead to "keeping one's head down" – as a soldier in a trench keeps their head down, for fear of being shot. Or an employee in a tough work environment who keeps their profile low to avoid being noticed by an irrational boss.

But Ibn Ata Allah has a non-fear-based reason for his advice: "what sprouts out of an unburied seed," he says, "will not yield good results." That is, an unburied seed may sprout for a moment, but it does not yield produce. It needs soil.

And burying oneself in the soil of insignificance means, I think, setting aside one's own preoccupations and judgements in order to experience the world exactly as it presents itself. As a manager, place to one side your own perceptions of how things *should* be – be insignificant enough to experience them as they are. What are your employees really saying and doing? What would they be saying and doing if, as it were, you were not there?

Moreover, such an attitude is probably in line with reality. We are less important than we believe. I knew an employee who threatened to leave their place of employment. This would be, he felt, a real loss to the employer. However, one of his colleagues said something like, "Consider someone who has their hand in a bucket of water. If the hand is removed, the water immediately and completely fills the space it previously occupied. The bucket has instantly recovered its equilibrium. The hand is not missed." Do we estimate correctly how quickly our organization, our colleagues and employees would recover should we leave?

So perhaps humility can help us see things as they are, and thus manage others better. And, like the seed in Ibn Ata Allah's aphorism, we can actually develop our own nature more effectively.

There would seem to be a couple of dangers in trying to manage with humility. First, the effort – perversely enough – can boomerang and become a source of pride. Some readers may recall novelist Charles Dickens' character Uriah Heep, who goes around boasting about being "so very 'umble." One wants to avoid hypocrisy; probably better to be boastful right up front than preening about being unassuming.

Second, sometimes one *needs* to promote oneself. I remember asking a colleague – regrettably, now departed – to review a draft statement that I wrote in support of my case for tenure. He read it with disapproval. "The whole point is," he said, "to make a case for yourself." I rewrote what I felt was a rather more boastful version. I guess it is like the question posed by first century rabbi Hillel the Elder: "If I am not for myself, who will be for me?"

But Rabbi Hillel also asked, "If I am only for myself, what am I?" Along those lines, burying ourselves in the ground of insignificance may be a key, if uncommon, managerial discipline.

Ibn Ata Allah al-Iskandari was born in Alexandria in the 13th century BCE, into a family of religious scholars. Initially drawn to Islamic jurisprudence, he moved to Cairo and taught there. There, too, he had a kind of conversion to Sufiism, a mystical dimension of Islam. He became a famous Sufi teacher; his *Kitab al-Hikam* or *Book of Aphorisms* is the source of the quote above.

Greenleaf, R. K. (1970). *The servant as leader*. Westfield, IN: Greenleaf Center for Servant Leadership.

Ibn Ata Allah al-Iskandari (2018). *The book of aphorisms: being a translation of Kitab al-Hikam*. Islamic Book Trust.

Mittal, R., & Dorfman, P. W. (2012). Servant leadership across cultures. *Journal of world Business*, *47*(4), 555-570.

7. Work and Labor

Some philosophers suggest that there is work, which can be uplifting, and labor, which is crushing. Are most of our days a mix?

> "Work is a good thing for man — a good thing for his humanity – because through work man *not only transforms nature,* adapting it to his own needs, but he also *achieves fulfillment* as a human being and indeed, in a sense, becomes 'more a human being'." – St. John Paul II
>
> "No one should ever work. Work is the source of nearly all the misery in the world. Almost any evil you'd care to name comes from working or from living in a world designed for work. In order to stop suffering, we have to stop working." – Bob Black

Above you have two rather different views of work. In the first, work is imagined as ennobling and humanizing. In the second it is pictured as the source of "nearly all misery." Which is it?

The case for each is relatively easy to make. Work is humanizing when we realize and ripen innate or developed capabilities. Work teaches us how to "transform nature" – for example, raw wood into a finished table. It also transforms us somehow, as we gain knowledge, learn skills, and take on and carry out responsibilities. In this vision of work, we are in some way accomplishing what we were designed to accomplish. In doing so, we begin to perceive who and even why we are.

In the second case, the figure of work is, simply, devastating. It is equivalent to suffering. And it is equivalent to suffering, presumably, because of its basically coercive nature: in virtually all circumstances, what we'd rather be doing is not working. By extrapolation, rather than work assisting us in becoming more human, it deforms us into being less human.

Managers have a unique perspective in which they may see both these realities. Most of us, I assume, would rather see employees ennobled rather than degraded by work. Hence our efforts to find the right kind and amount of work for them, to understand their limits so we can help them avoid burnout, to recognize their potential, challenge them, and help guide their development. And as attitudes toward work change toward a world where work is simply less central in our lives, managers are able to adapt so that the most fruitful dimensions of work are stressed.

At the same time, managers can sometimes see the negative effects of work on their employees. They can see those who are struggling to adapt to deadlines and accomplish assignments. They can see when life events outside work make work itself a great burden. Sometimes, even, managers perceive (clearly or dimly) that they themselves are regarded as a source of suffering. It may not be overly troubling just to be disliked, but it may be uncomfortable to consider that dislike to be justified in some ways by one's own attitudes and actions.

Moreover, unlike some employees, managers typically both have bosses above them, and at the same time are themselves bosses to others. In this way, they can understand the negative impacts of work through their own experiences of the exercise of power upon them. It is even possible that the possession and utilization of power can be dangerous, quite aside from having anyone above you. Simone Weil seems to suggest this when she wrote, "Power contains a sort of fatality which weighs as pitilessly on those who command as on those who obey."

So how do we think about work: is it good, bad, or both? One way to ponder this is to talk about "labor" on the one hand, and "work" on the other. This was philosopher's Hannah Arendt's approach. In *The Human Condition* she points out that in labor, people are driven into a life of "repetition and the endlessness of the process itself." Work, on the other hand, is what St. John Paul II was referring to: workers who freely associate, and who create new value through transforming the world.

Repetitive, difficult, draining labor might be associated with old images of a factory, with its pace-setting assembly lines – as in Charlie Chaplin's *Modern Times*. But what was modern in *Modern Times* is still modern. In today's factories, those timed assembly lines still exist, even if the labor is assisted by robots.

Years ago, I worked loading boxes onto trucks in a UPS facility. The conveyer belt drove the speed at which I worked. Recently one of my children worked in a similar job for FedEx Ground– his experience was identical. A job like this, and jobs at warehouses such as those run by Amazon, can be difficult if not impossible to sustain over time. Such work may be suitable for the short-term, but over longer time such employment gradually morphs into *labor*, with Arendt's "repetition and endlessness."

Work in Arendt's sense, though, evokes the craftsperson. In this kind of activity, there is an autonomy to decide the tasks one accomplishes and the order in which they are accomplished. There is control, maybe, over the environment in which the work is done. Schedules can be set or altered as desired. It is, in short, humanizing rather than otherwise, an upper not a downer.

In real, non-idealized life we can expect to see both aspects, work and labor, in our jobs and in the jobs of those we manage. We would do well to aspire to work, rather than labor. The great thing is that as managers we have some freedom to create more work, less labor, for employees. And for ourselves.

St. John Paul II (Karol Józef Wojtyła; 1920-2005) was the 264th Pope of the Catholic Church, and one of the longest serving (26 years). He released the encyclical "On Human Work" in 1981; he was canonized in 2014.

Robert Charles "Bob" Black, Jr. (b. 1951) is an anarchist thinker and writer, who imagines a post-work world.

Arendt, H. (2013). *The human condition*. University of Chicago press.

Black, B. (1986). *The abolition of work and other essays*. Port Townsend, WA: Loompanics Unlimited.

Catholic Church. Pope John Paul II. (1981). *On human work: encyclical Laborem exercens*. Washington, D.C. (1312 Massachusetts Ave., N.W., Washington 20005): Office of Publishing Services, United States Catholic Conference.

Weil, S. (2001). *Oppression and Liberty*. Translated by Arthur Willis and John Petrie. New York: Routledge.

Zaretsky, R., & Alliger, G.M. (2023). The crucial difference between labor and work. *Boston Globe*, April.

8. Who Are You When Not Managing?

A Roman emperor has some good words on action and identity

"In your actions, don't procrastinate. In your conversations, don't confuse. In your thoughts, don't wander. In your soul, don't be passive or aggressive. In your life, don't be all about business." – Marcus Aurelius

Marcus Aurelius was a Stoic philosopher, not to mention an emperor. The quote above has much that speaks directly to any manager. Don't procrastinate in your job duties, don't confuse your employees when talking to them, focus your thoughts and attention on your job, and maintain a balanced attitude – be a good listener but also be as proactive and firm as required. Aurelius' last words, however – "In your life, don't be all about business" – strike a rather modern note about living a life that is not just about work.

I recall a *New Yorker* cartoon in which a family – mother, father, and children – are sitting around the kitchen table; presumably dinner is just completed. The father says to the children, "I'm going to have to let some of you go."

The absurdity of it is appealing; the father has so taken on his work persona as boss that he treats the family like a business – to the extent that the children, like employees, can be cast off when circumstances require it. Of course, some families really have members ready to get rid of each other – that is not so funny.

For our purposes, though, we can use (my memory of) the cartoon to highlight a real question: who are you when not the boss at work?

It has long been noted that "workism" – the valorization of work as the primary activity and even primary purpose of life – characterizes modern life, particularly in the United States. This societal emphasis can lead not just to work-life imbalances, but even to the creation and persistence of jobs that are functionally useless. Most importantly, though, the societal centralization of work seems to raise questions about who we are when not at work.

It would appear from numerous polls that the desire to maintain a good work-life balance has been increasing in the United States. Such a balance between work and the rest of life can be understood in multiple ways. Management researchers Thomas Kalliath and Paula Brough point out that an overall work-life balance includes balancing *time*, balancing *involvement*, and balancing *satisfaction* across home and work roles. It can also be viewed as a lack of *conflict* between these roles. These authors suggest a definition: "Work-life balance is the individual perception that work and non-work activities are compatible and promote growth in accordance with an individual's current life priorities."

But I think also that work-life balance depends in large part on one underexamined concept: that of nonwork identity. We ought to be anchored, first, in our nonwork self. This nonwork self begins to develop before we ever start working. It is an *essential* identity that work can modify but should not be allowed to coopt.

If we refuse to let work take on such an outsized role that we forget who we were prior to entering work, then we have a centered personality while we work. And, when retiring from work we can easily lay aside the trappings of a career. It is thus our identity outside of work that defines whether and how we succeed – or not – in allowing work to take a reasonable and satisfactory place in our lives.

Let's say that *work identity* is the degree to which a person defines themselves by their job with all its relationships, activities and duties, challenges, and opportunities. *Nonwork identity* is then the extent to which the outside-of-work relationships, activities and duties, interests, challenges, and opportunities in the family, neighborhood, and community are felt to be central to how a person understands themselves.

For each person, either of these identities can be weak or strong. This gives rise to four possible combinations, as illustrated in the table below.

		Work Identity	
		Weak	Strong
Nonwork Identity	Weak	• Low Work Centrality • Passive, unactivated • Lack of defined "self"	• High Work Centrality • Psychologically challenged when no work
	Strong	• Low Work Centrality • Fine with transitions or periods of no work	• Moderate Work Centrality • Autonomous Self – Fine with and without work

Let's assume one has strong Work Identify and but weak Nonwork Identity (upper right in table). In this case "Work Centrality" – the degree to which work plays a key role in life – is likely to be high. But people falling in that quadrant are likely to be challenged if no jobs are available. In this case, life satisfaction can suffer. We do in fact often find strong negative effects of unemployment, during prime working years, upon life satisfaction. That this is the case for many makes sense, not just because of probable financial difficulties, but because of the already noted strong valorization of work in our societies. Interestingly, satisfaction among the unemployed increases when they finally retire from work – that is, they are no longer looking for or expecting work. And researcher Ruth Mcfadyen argued that how one *categorizes oneself* (that is, what identity one takes on) when unemployed affects the ability to deal with stigmas associated with unemployment. For example, an identity of "unemployed" would be inferior to an identity of "caretaker" or "house husband". For these latter have a strong Nonwork Identity. Similarly, a person whose Nonwork Identity is weak but who has strong Work Identity could be a candidate for workaholism.

If both Nonwork and Work Identity is weak (upper left in table), then the individual will be passive – unlikely either to seek out meaningful work or to find meaning at home or leisure. Such people are unlikely to be bothered by unemployment.

I would make the argument that you can be a better manager if you have a strong Nonwork Identity, whether your Work Identity is strong or weak. The basic thought is that you are a person first, outside of work. Then you can enter the working world and either also fully identify with that, or not identify with it so strongly. Even in this latter case, though, your Nonwork Identity will infuse your management so that, even if you are not working extra hours, you know who you are and can manage from that centered point.

Marcus Aurelius Antoninus (121-180) was Roman Emperor from 161-180. His Stoic writings in his *Meditations* are justly famous. He survived many battles as well as a brutal plague during the 160s.

Kalliath, T., & Brough, P. (2008). Work–life balance: A review of the meaning of the balance construct. *Journal of Management & Organization, 14(3)*, 323-327.

McFadyen, R. G. (1995). Coping with threatened identities: Unemployed people's self-categorizations. *Current Psychology, 14*, 233-256.

Ter Bogt, T., Raaijmakers, Q., & Van Wel, F. (2005). Socialization and development of the work ethic among adolescents and young adults. *Journal of Vocational Behavior, 66(3)*, 420-437.

9. A Burning That Leaves No Trace

Three views of the close interactions between ourselves and our world

"Education is the kindling of a flame, not the filling of a vessel." – Socrates

"When you do something, you should burn yourself completely, like a good bonfire, leaving no trace of yourself." – Soto Zen monk Shunryū Suzuki

"Everything that touches you shall burn you, and you will draw your hand away in pain, until you have withdrawn yourself from all things." – Trappist monk Thomas Merton

The above quotes image a range of combustions: From the kindling flame of education, to the flame that consumes the actor, to the one that causes complete detachment.

Socrates is an historic but almost unknowable character. Since he left no writings, historians and philosophers both try to discern his real person and teachings in the writings of others, such as Xenophon, Plato and Aristotle. Still, from his military service, to his impact on both his contemporary peers and modern audiences, to his insouciance toward his own death, he has achieved a kind of mythic standing in the West.

What might Socrates' (unfortunately probably apocryphal) statement, "Education is the kindling of a flame, not the filling of a vessel," mean? Most obviously, it suggests that collecting facts is not education. Nor, presumably, is education simply the learning of procedures. Somehow facts and procedures need to become living, creating warmth for ourselves and others, as a fire.

In our organizational training, both that we attend as managers and promote for employees, Socrates' quote stands as a kind of challenge. Is the training just a filling of a bucket? Or is a flame somehow kindled, a flame that would indicate real interest and curiosity grabbing the trainee?

What percent of the training, would you say, that you have had in your career so far is just the filling of a vessel, what percent kindling of a fire?

Importantly, Socrates is implying that education will transform you in some fundamental way. The original you – your experiences, knowledge, and even being – provides the material which is eaten up. Learning through burning. Good training and development leave you different than you were. It might even be said that it is not without personal cost – some of you is consumed as fuel in the process.

This brings us almost seamlessly to Shunryū Suzuki's thought: "When you do something, you should burn yourself completely, like a good bonfire, leaving no trace of yourself." Suzuki was a Soto (quiet school) Zen monk in the first half of the 20th century. Many were the difficulties he faced in pursuing his dream, first of becoming a Zen monk, and second, of bringing Zen to the United States. He succeeded in both, but needed to go through rigorous training and difficult experiences to do so.

Burn yourself completely when you do something, so that no trace of yourself is left. Rather than education as in Socrates' thought, here action is the focus. What might it mean to act so that no trace of yourself is left?

At this point you might interrupt to say, "what manager wants to leave no trace of themselves?" Good point. I recall my first real stint in the business world, at a large training facility of a major technology company. What struck me in the first few months was how many of the managers seemed to want precisely to create traces of themselves – to make a mark. To this end they hired consultants of various ilk to help push through pet projects. As a relative outsider, it was clear to me that these projects often overlapped in purpose. But it turned out that this was an impolitic point to make, for each manager wanted the project to be clearly associated with him or her. It wasn't perhaps so much about getting things done as making a name.

What a different attitude from this, to simply put your all into your work – to the extent that, in a sense, you are consumed and nothing is left. Who does this? Only a minority, I venture. But you will occasionally find such managers, who care more for the outcome of a project than for their reputation.

Mightn't there be something freeing indeed in plunging into work to such an extent? If one of the central problems of our current time is self-consciousness, what better way to forget oneself? Not to mention, of course, the outcome of the work itself. Quality is more likely, it seems to me, if one gives one's all. And in such a case, it may actually be that the end of the effort – success or failure – is not important, since it was not about oneself to start with.

Last, consider the seemingly dire statement by Thomas Merton: "Everything that touches you shall burn you, and you will draw your hand away in pain, until you have withdrawn yourself from all things."

Merton was a convert to Catholicism, and became a Trappist monk (the Trappists are also known as the Order of Cistercians of the Strict Observance). Spending much solitary time in a hermitage on monastery grounds, Merton, like Suzuki, went through difficult as well as good times. He became an author of many books and is well-known in certain circles for his writings on contemplation. Interestingly, he took an active interest in, and wrote about, Eastern religions – and Christianity in relation to these.

The quote from Merton is actually an excerpt of a kind of visionary statement about himself. It is he, Merton, who will be burned, experience pain, and need to withdraw "from all things." But this process of encountering a burning reality is really just part of what makes a contemplative out of an ordinary seeker. It is the reactive counterpart to "all things are vanity." No thing can satisfy – instead it will *not* satisfy; and more than that, it will even cause a kind of burning pain.

This thought, of the three, is hardest to apply to managers. It will probably apply only to a few. But if taken to heart in the right way, it will mean this: all the bad things you experience in your job – the unnecessary meetings; the obsequious, prickly, or resentful employees; the competition and grasping of other managers; the failures to advance – can act as spurs to rethink. To rethink in some deep way who you are and where, really, you are going.

Socrates (circa 470-399 BCE) was an Athenian philosopher who greatly influenced his contemporaries. He died from a poison administered after he was convicted of corrupting Athenian youth.

Shunryū Suzuki (1904-1971). Suzuki, unlike many Japanese Zen proponents, was not a vociferous supporter of the Japanese war movement in WWII.

Thomas Merton (1915-1968), wrote many books on spiritual topics, including his influential autobiography *The Seven Storey Mountain*. He died through accidental electrocution while visiting Asia.

Merton, T. (1999). *The seven storey mountain*. Houghton Mifflin Harcourt.

Suzuki, Shunryu (1970). *Zen mind, beginner's mind*. Weatherhill.

10. Boredom and Work

Most of us don't like being bored – work can help us

"Work saves us from three great evils: boredom, vice and need." - Voltaire

Most people hate boredom. They also hate need: hunger, thirst, too much heat, too much cold, lacking funds. Whether vice is hated is another question. Probably this is because the most potent and unpleasant meanings of the word "vice" have been squeezed out; instead we talk of "vices." Vices are those small, almost endearing habits which we each will correct some time in our future: smoking, drinking rather too much, excessive sleeping in, lying, the not-so-subtle comatosing of our minds via YouTube or Netflix.

But vice in its primal state refers to the kinds of depravity and wickedness that witness to actual corruption in our innermost selves. If work can save us from this kind of vice, how powerful a palliative it must be.

Rather than vice or need, however, let's here consider work's role in saving us from boredom.

Boredom is an affective, that is, emotional, state characterized by an unpleasant awareness of the passage of time due to a lack of directed activity.

For researchers, boredom is not the same as monotony. Monotony is a lack of variation in stimuli. Monotony often does, but need not, cause boredom. For example, a job which seems very monotonous on the surface to most people may still be found sufficiently interesting to some. This may be because they need little stimulation, or – more intriguingly – they perceive small, interesting differences and variations where others don't. Monotony thus can translate into boredom, or be experienced, seemingly paradoxically, as interesting. As Simone Weil pointed out, monotony is either "the sign of unvarying perpetuity... time sterilized," or "a reflection of eternity... time surpassed."

To help think about boredom, the so-called "Affect Circumplex" is presented below. Two continua are presented: Unpleasant to Pleasant, and Low to High Activation. These allow us to categorize some common emotions and experiences in terms of how these dimensions interact.

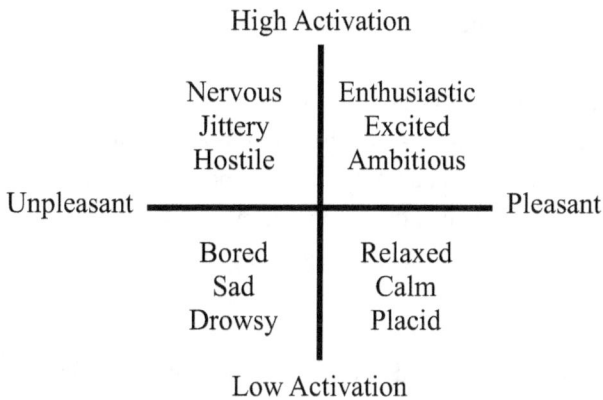

High Activation

	Nervous	Enthusiastic	
	Jittery	Excited	
	Hostile	Ambitious	
Unpleasant			Pleasant
	Bored	Relaxed	
	Sad	Calm	
	Drowsy	Placid	

Low Activation

"Activation" represents a combination of the physiological and the psychological. When highly activated, we are usually ready to act or continue acting.

If we are activated and in a pleasant state (upper right quadrant), we are ready to work, to accomplish. Pleasant activation on the job is synonymous with engagement. This is a desirable state, for it is here that tasks are accomplished. The "goodness" of this state presumes, of course, that the organization's larger goals are themselves desirable. Even malicious hackers can be pleasantly activated.

When we are activated but things seem unpleasant (upper left quadrant), we may be ready to act defensively or aggressively. In some cases, we may be worried about what we should do – we are jittery or nervous. Employees may evince this state in the case of uncertainties such as lack of direction in their work or lack of resources to accomplish that work. One of the jobs of managers is to ensure that employees occupy as little time as possible in this distressing upper left quadrant.

The lower right quadrant signifies low activation and a pleasant emotional state. Here we experience peace and rest. It seems important for employees to periodically ramp down and relax. Sometimes it is in exactly such states that insights occur; creativity may be boosted by "stepping back" from work demands and details. Allowing employees such recollective time seems a good idea.

Now to the quadrant of most interest for us at the moment: the lower left. Low activation, unpleasant; it is here that boredom and listlessness can be found. Employees faced with highly repetitive work or insufficient work, lack of autonomy, and/or monotony of whatever kind may be bored. This is the opposite of engagement; it is disengagement of an aversive sort.

Work, Voltaire says, should save one from the evil of boredom. But alas, it may not do so without the proper characteristics: tasks that vary in their demands (that is, draw upon different skills); tasks that stretch us to the limits of our knowledge and capabilities; tasks that somehow contribute to a larger outcome; tasks that allow us to understand how well we are performing; tasks that bring us into contact with valued colleagues and clients.

The "worker's philosopher" Eric Hoffer agrees with Voltaire:

> The differentiated individual is free of boredom only when he is
> engaged either in creative work or some absorbing occupation or

when he is wholly engrossed in the struggle for existence. Pleasure-chasing and dissipation are ineffective palliatives.

Here it's clear that, for Hoffer, vice is not a useful replacement for work. Struggling to exist (Voltaire's "need") may be. But it seems that by far the best alternative is that upper right quadrant, where employees can be "absorbed" and "engrossed." If ensuring this experience for workers seems a high bar for management, it is: it is the holy grail of an "engaged" workforce.

Incidentally, when Hoffer refers to "the differentiated individual," he is using a concept popularized by Carl Jung. Psychological differentiation is the process, and the outcome of the process, whereby a particular person discovers the meaning of who they are. They are then "differentiated," both within themselves (understanding themselves as complex entities), and amongst others (understanding themselves as unique).

Work researchers Carina Schott and Caroline Fischer propose that boredom can be an advantageous state for employees – that boredom has a "bright side." This is because it may offer opportunities. These include: bored workers may be particularly ready to accept company training; it can be explained to bored workers that their jobs are, after all useful to the company and society, so that at least they experience a sense of employment meaningfulness; boring jobs may present opportunities for managers to offer greater decision-making authority to those in such jobs – thus reducing boredom; if a job is boring it may be ripe for the addition of additional tasks.

One can add to this that, if in a given job only some employees are bored, a manager might look at those that are bored. Are they perhaps bored because their capabilities are not being used and, in fact, they might be ready for advancement? In this sense boredom can be a signal for talent succession management.

A final, more radical proposal might be made for those jobs that workers experience as boring. This would be to provide an extra-large space for job crafting by employees. Job crafting is a granting of management-like autonomy and power to employees. David Frayne, for example, suggests that "Genuine autonomy consists in a freedom to have a say in what is being produced, and for whose benefit. It consists in a freedom to question the authenticity and the importance of the needs that work is designed to meet." I guess this would mean that one way to fight employee boredom is to offer them real power. Maybe put them on the company board (pun intended?)!

> Voltaire (François-Marie Arouet; 1694-1778), was a writer, philosopher, and wit. He parodied many of the people, movements, and institutions of his day.

Frayne, D. (2015). *The refusal of work: The theory and practice of resistance to work*. Bloomsbury Publishing.

Hoffer, E. (1951). *The true believer*. Mentor.

Russell, J. A. (1980). A circumplex model of affect. *Journal of Personality and Social Psychology, 39*(6), 1161.

Schott, C., & Fischer, C. (2023). How to turn workplace boredom into something positive. A theoretical framework of the 'bright sides' of boredom. *Human Resource Management Review, 33(2)*, 100952.

Voltaire, F. (2013). *Candide, or optimism*. Penguin UK.

Weil, S. (1997). *Gravity and grace*. U of Nebraska Press.

11. Attention I: Attention and Listening

Can work actually be purifying?

"Every time that we truly pay attention, we destroy evil in ourselves... a quarter of an hour of attention is very good work." – Simone Weil

French philosopher and profound mystic Simone Weil, quoted above, was a contemporary of two other notable French citizens during the last century. The first, Pierre Teilhard de Chardin, was a paleontologist, Jesuit, and also a mystic. Jean-Paul Sartre, on the other hand, was a playwright, novelist, a founder of existentialism, and confirmed atheist (at least – according to some accounts – until just prior to his death). I mention Teilhard and Sartre because these very different people were, according to reports, very alike in one respect: they listened with an intensity that surprised and even stunned others.

You may have had similar experiences to those who spoke with Teilhard or Sartre. You have been speaking for a while with someone. Then it suddenly strikes you that the other is actually *listening*. It can take one aback, so rare is this ability. Rare because it requires real attention which is, as Weil says, work.

What may we say about attention and managers? Certainly, managers employ attention in many ways throughout any given workday. Visually, they may study documents, displays, and data of various kinds. Physically, they may attend to tasks using keyboards or machines. And they almost certainly communicate with employees and other managers, whether face-to-face or remotely. To do any of these activities demands attention. But how many managers pay attention *well* is a question.

First, you may ask another question: what is attention anyway? It turns out that although researchers have attended closely to human attention since the founding of psychology, they have failed notably in fully answering this question. Psychologist Donald Broadbent is famous for looking into visual attention. It is, he said, like a searchlight or spotlight. The searchlight can move focus from one object to another, and narrow its beam as required in order to obtain maximum detail. Other psychologists stress that attention should be understood as a servant of action. When you as a manager need to rank tasks by priority, that places demands on you, which in turn guides how you direct your attention. In any case, instead of a unified theory of attention, there are a multitude of approaches to partially understanding it; there are cognitive, neurophysiological, and even mathematical angles. And as mentioned, we can pay attention visually, manually or tactilely, and auditorily.

Let's focus for a moment on auditory attention, that is, listening to other people (although listening in many cases involves vision and body language, hence visual and physical attention as well). For managers listening is a crucial skill, although managers are under-trained in it. And listening in the workplace is also under-studied. There is evidence, though, from some research which suggests that good listening by managers is related to employee trust, job knowledge, job performance, well-being, and even turnover intentions.

Interestingly, researchers Avraham Kluger and Guy Itzchakov suggest that attention is fundamentally an antecedent to listening. It manifests itself in observable behaviors of two different types. What they call Backchannel Behaviors are non-verbal acts of attention for the most part, and include body posture, facial expression, nodding, and gaze, but also laughing, and exclaiming. Verbal Communication is the second type, including paraphrasing, repeating, questions, naming emotions, and so forth.

When manager attention demonstrates itself both via Backchannel (non-verbal) Behaviors and Verbal Communication, these researchers point out, it creates a kind of virtuous cycle. The employee perceives real listening and develops a sense of psychological safety. This in turn leads to less defensiveness and more honest disclosure. It can happen too that this response leads the manager herself to relax and be more open. I would further speculate that under these conditions, workplace "contracts" then feel less impersonal and in a sense less rigorous; the employee may gain a sense of greater autonomy. And perceived autonomy is a crucial part of the bedrock of job satisfaction.

It would seem then that we really ought to be teaching managers to listen carefully. Can we do that? To some extent. For example, paraphrasing an employee's words (or "active listening") can be taught and is an effective technique. And perhaps non-verbal cues such as nodding or smiling can be learned. But this angle is a bit thorny. For non-verbal communication, as anthropologist and linguist Edward Sapir pointed out, seems to occur "in accordance with an elaborate and secret code that is written nowhere, known by none, and understood by all." This suggests that sincere listening attention may be difficult to learn, critical organizational resource though it may be. It is certainly almost impossible to fake.

Not only is it difficult to fake, but it is easily disrupted. That our powers of concentration are under general attack is, I think, well known. Whether it's the insistent dinging of text messages or the siren call of the internet, we are now living in a world where activities requiring sustained attention are undermined.

This brings us back to Simone Weil's belief that true attention transforms the attender. If she is correct, then the manager who strives to listen to, to be present with, her employees will reap a double benefit. Not only will there be desirable work outcomes for the employees and the organization, but the manager herself will be altered – will recognize psychological and perhaps soulful benefits – via the practice of attention.

Simone Weil (1909-1943) led a short, intense life. Born into a Jewish French family, she is known for her crystalline philosophic writing and Christian theology. A strong advocate of workers, Weil tried desperately to get physically engaged in important conflicts of her time, for instance as a fighter in the Spanish Revolution or in the French resistance during WWII. However, her physical infirmities prevented this.

Kluger, A. N., & Itzchakov, G. (2022). The power of listening at work. *Annual Review of Organizational Psychology and Organizational Behavior*, 9, 121-146.

Sapir, E. (1927). *The unconscious patterning of behavior in society*. In D. G. Mandelbaum (Ed.), Selected writings of Edward Sapir (pp. 544–559). Berkley: University of California Press.

Weil, S. (2009). *Waiting on God* (Routledge Revivals). Routledge.

12. Attention II: Transcending the Everyday (Occasionally)

Why do we tend to fall out of wondering?

> It is easy to live each day in "a cloud of commonplace interpretation." – G.K. Chesterton

In the ordinary course of events, human consciousness is dampened or limited. This is true across any number of domains of functioning, from low-level sensory awareness to our most complex cognitive or emotional experiences.

We tend to go about our days, including our days at work, in states of awareness that vary along a continuum of everydayness. If there were pointers on our foreheads that indicated the state of our awareness, rarely would it inch into that out-of-normal zone where the unusual is experienced. In his essay "Lamp-Posts," G.K. Chesterton illustrates how an ordinary object, a lamppost, can be viewed by a child as wonderfully extraordinary. Or, it can be viewed within the "cloud of the commonplace" by a statistician, who sees it only as one ordinary item among many ordinary items.

In fact, the daily lives of managers are usually, well, routine and rather ordinary. We move from seeing, doing, hearing, and saying one thing to seeing, doing, hearing, and saying another without a sense of moving into or through anything particularly unusual. The tasks we face, the employees with whom we deal, are – as we think – understood by us. We seem to perceive things as they are and accept that perception.

This moving through the world as if the essence of things in that world can largely be ignored, is, I think, simply adaptive. Since I do need to have meetings and write emails – perhaps several of each before 10 a.m. – being continually agog at the very nature of the world would not be particularly helpful for business. Rather, I need to execute all those automatic mental programs and physical routines that allow me to get something done while thinking of the next thing that needs to get done. This is a big reason for the "cloud of the commonplace": our acting and accomplishing would be profoundly hindered if we were always in a state of heightened consciousness, continually recognizing the inner light of people and things.

In trying to describe why we ordinarily live in only the ordinary, a word mentioned above – "dampen" –may be useful. This is because it seems likely that there is a kind of inhibitory or suppressive and unconscious mechanism which operates at a biological level, and which keeps really unusual states of awareness at bay. Perhaps "inhibit" and "suppress" have negative connotations to the modern mind, but in this case they are not meant to carry that weight. Rather, much inhibition is an automatic, unconscious, low-level activity which permits an entity to go about living or accomplishing. Consider in this regard what cognitive psychologists call "selective attention." A person attends to something, and to do that successfully, competing stimuli are suppressed. You may know a person, for example, who when reading will miss great chunks of auditory input – even voices directed right at her. Or you may be such a person. In these cases, the auditory function is adaptively inhibited so that printed words can be processed by visual and intellectual subsystems. This inhibition is accomplished without awareness or conscious effort. Indeed, conscious efforts at inhibition are likely to backfire, as in the case of a manager trying too hard to avoid bad presentation technique.

So we are lucky that we have inhibitory biopsychological systems that function to keep us grounded in everyday reality. The frontal cortex of the human brain often plays a role in generating these adaptive inhibitions. But as Harvard researchers Daniel Dillon and Diego Pizzagalli point out, the neurophysiology of inhibition varies, depending on its focus – whether emotions, actions, or attention are being supported through inhibition of competing processes. Interestingly, neurological dysfunction – "inhibitory deficits" – in these dampening abilities of the brain may underlie psychopathologies of different types. Schizophrenia, for example, is associated with diminished functioning in the frontal part of the brain. Without terming ADHD a pathology, we can nonetheless note that this diagnosis too is often associated with diminished response inhibition.

So inhibitory processes, most often unconscious, are characteristics of normal people, in normal states of consciousness. We might even say that these dampening processes keep us in our usual, non-transcendent state of awareness.

But, in a surprise, it may also be a kind of inhibition that permits transcendence. Specifically, what if the sense of self is itself inhibited? It turns out that it is this which may underlie those rare, otherworldly states of consciousness where we are aware of something greater than ourselves. In a series of experiments, psychologist Patrick Lin and colleagues suggested to subjects ("primed" the subjects with) the concept of God. They found, regardless of religious affiliation, whether the priming was overt or subliminal, whether with student subjects or working adult subjects, that such priming reduced, or inhibited, self-orientation. This suggests, they conclude, "a possible mechanism for self-transcendence." In a way, these researchers are saying that the self can get in the way of greater awareness, can restrict experiences and perceptions that are unusual. It's reasonable to conclude that prayer and meditation, then, act to dampen self-orientation and allow a greater awareness.

And many have suggested that experiences of the transcendent have a particular power to change us. You may have had a singular experience of something greater than yourself – of transcendence – that has had a lasting impact on you.

Management training does not focus on the transcendent. Nor should it, since it's not clear how much learning of management techniques can occur when one is in a profound meditative state.

But perhaps transcendence can mean that place where Chesterton's "cloud of commonplace interpretation" is temporarily set aside for a broader, more global awareness of the amazing character of people and things as they exist in themselves. The *flavor* of this overarching perception or sense of value could persist without damaging effectiveness. It could even infuse a manager's life, and hence her posture toward employees and others in the workplace.

Gilbert K. Chesterton (1874-1936) was a prolific and popular British speaker and author; he created the famous mystery-solving character of Father Brown.

Chesterton, G. K. (1921). *The uses of diversity.* Dodd, Mead and Company.

Dillon, D. G., & Pizzagalli, D. A. (2007). Inhibition of action, thought, and emotion: a selective neurobiological review. *Applied and Preventive Psychology*, *12*(3), 99-114.

Lin, P. K., Ramsay, J. E., Chan, K. Q., Leow, Y. J., Lim, B. Y., & Tong, E. M. (2022). Self-transcendence through self-inhibition?: God primes reduce self-accessibility. *Psychology of Religion and Spirituality*, *14*(1), 31.

13. Attention III: Flow

Pure absorption in a task is pure joy, as Confucious knew

> Confucius said, "Why didn't you tell him that I am a man who forgets to eat when he is enthusiastic about something, who forgets all his worries when he is happy, and who is not aware that old age is coming on?"

A re you a person who might forget to eat when enthusiastically tackling a task at work? Do you have subordinates who are like that? The word for this experience is "flow." Flow is a desirable state where work is not work. What's great about this topic is that a lot of research has been done on it, including what it is, exactly, and how managers can facilitate it in the workplace.

Flow is usually thought of as an individual, subjective experience. It occurs when someone who is engaged in a task: is "lost" in the work (there is a sense of self-forgetfulness); time seems to stand still or move slowly; there is a sense of enjoyment, concentration, and control. It is accompanied by a feeling of being rewarded by the task in and of itself. The combination of these experiences has been termed "flow."

Although the concept was named and research initiated on it by academic Mihaly Csikszentmihalyi in 1975, the actual experience of flow must be as old as humankind. Consider Confucius' quote above. One of his acquaintances apparently did not know what to say when asked by another person to describe Confucius. Perhaps irked, perhaps amused, Confucious said, "Why didn't you tell him that I am a man who forgets to eat when he is enthusiastic about something, who forgets all his worries when he is happy, and who is not aware that old age is coming on?"

The first part of this quote, as we have said, epitomizes the flow experience – absorption, full attention, and enjoyment. (The other parts of Confucius' self-description we won't go into, although doesn't his insistence that he is not aware of old age approaching seem to imply precisely that he *is* aware of it?)

Given that the experience of flow at work is a kind of task satisfaction raised to the nth power, it seems natural to wonder how we can create the conditions for it, both for ourselves and for employees.

It is first important to note that setting up situations where it may occur for us or others does not guarantee that it *will* occur. We can increase the possibility of flow but to some extent it is beyond our power to ensure it. This is the case because of its numerous antecedents, which include some not in our control. For example, there are some physiological prerequisites, such as being at least somewhat rested. And the presence of profound, concentration-destroying concerns and worries can severely limit the likelihood of flow.

But there is a lot that managers can do; we can spell this out in four broad steps or factors.

First, *specific and clear goals and task structure* are important. It's been known for a long while that specific, difficult goals increase performance, but they are necessary for flow too. This makes sense: vague instructions are not particularly motivating.

Second, it is critical to *know how one is progressing in the task*. This is usually called task *feedback*.

Third, create a work environment where *unneeded interruptions are eliminated*. Concentration is difficult to develop if one needs to continually resurface, as it were, from the depths of task engagement.

Finally, and most fascinating, it is necessary that there be a *match or balance between employee skills, on the one hand, and task demands, on the other*. Specifically, if a worker's skills fit the task demands, flow may occur. Note that this "fit" can be reframed in terms of *challenge*. That is, it is not that a worker can easily do the task, "with her eyes closed," as it were. Rather, the demands of the task should be such that the worker can do it, but not without full engagement of attention and capabilities. It should be challenging, though not ultimately impossible.

So, as a manager, are you able to set up tasks with clear, specific goals? Obviously – this is simply one of the central duties of management. Are you able to provide timely feedback on task progression? Again, yes, you should be doing that. Of course, many tasks have in-built feedback mechanisms – a coder can often tell how well a particular assignment is going (for example by running automated unit tests); a bricklayer can see how many rows of bricks have been put in place. Can you reduce task interruptions?

And, can you ensure that an employee's task demands the sufficient amount of skill employment, but without making the task too hard? This is tougher. Remember that flow is subjective. You will need to ask your workers whether and to what extent they are experiencing flow. This, especially with new employees, may require frequent (but not too frequent!) check-ins. As Falko Rheinberg and colleagues discuss, some statements that indicate employee flow include: I feel just the right amount of challenge; I am totally absorbed in what I am doing; I do not notice time passing; My thoughts/activities run fluidly and smoothly; I feel that I have everything under control.

When determining the appropriate level of task demand so that an employee feels challenged but not overwhelmed, the nature of task difficulty needs to be considered. Difficulty can be affected by task dimensions such as novelty, complexity, deadlines, amount to be accomplished, and the presence of other, competing tasks. And all these interact with the skill level of the employee.

And then there is the difficulty of knowing how to ramp up task demands appropriately as an employee develops ever greater skill and knowledge. Again, this implies the need to really be "in tune" with your workers.

Another wrinkle in managing employees so that flow is maximized is that of personality (not skill) differences among workers. Csikszentmihalyi himself didn't doubt that some individuals were predisposed to engage in flow. He called these people *autotelic* (from the Greek *auto*, self, and *telos*, goal). Autotelic personalities not only desire the experience of flow, but somehow perceive how to manage it. They discern both their skills and also tasks that can challenge those skills. In a sense, they are able to set up a work world where work is more apt, for them, to be like play.

One interesting aspect of autotelic personalities is that they are low in fear of failure. Instead, they have high NAch – need for achievement. Thus, challenging work is attractive to them, for it provides a field for engagement and possible success. Those who fear failure, on the other hand, may well pick less challenging tasks so that their own valued outcome – not failing – is likely to be met.

So this is a "wrinkle" in managing for flow because some workers may simply prefer easier, non-challenging tasks. They are non-autotelic. You may need to sort employees in your own mind into the self-motivated, high NAch, on the one hand, and the less motivated, on the other.

The experience of flow at work is pleasurable to experience and good to witness. And if an employee is ever so deeply engaged in their work that you need to encourage them to take a break or eat lunch, you may have a Confucius on your hands.

Confucius (Kong Qui; circa 551-479 BCE), was a foundational Chinese philosopher. He promoted morality, family unity and veneration of ancestors, sincerity, and justice. For him, ceremonies acted to link individuals to the past and to public virtue.

Lin, Y. T. (1966). *Wisdom of Confucius*. New York: Modern Library.

Rheinberg, F., Vollmeyer, R., & Engeser, S. (2003). Die Erfassung des Flow-Erlebens [The assessment of flow experience]. In J. Stiensmeier-Pelster & F. Rheinberg (Eds.), *Diagnostik von Selbstkonzept, Lernmotivation und Selbstregulation [Diagnosis of motivation and self-concept]* (pp. 261–279). Gottingen: Hogrefe.

14. Performance Management I: The Parable of the Bricks

Physicist Max Planck's thoughts on the effects of measurement can illumine the assessment of employee performance

> "Measurement has a more or less causal influence on the very process that is under observation." – Max Planck

One of the obvious duties of any manager is to guide employees. To do that, it seems necessary to understand how employees are performing their jobs, in terms of both quality and quantity of output.

Because of this apparent need to assess performance, measurements and targets are required. In the modern workplace, this aspect of management is called Performance Management. Performance Management includes setting performance goals, measuring or keeping track of performance (such as rating and/or ranking), providing feedback, identifying good and poor performers, and making decisions based on assessed performance (e.g., promotion, rewards, development opportunities, performance improvement plans).

But measurement of job performance is fraught with problems. Work researchers have long examined the nature of such problems. Some of these problems are more or less established and easy to grasp, while others – like the one alluded to by Max Planck in the quote above – are less fully understood.

Researchers sometimes call measures of job performance "criteria." In addition to possibly creating unwanted effects, criteria can, and often are, flawed. They can be "unreliable," "contaminated," "deficient," and "biased." Managers should be aware of each of these possibilities, so we discuss each briefly below.

An *unreliable* measure is one that does not give the same result each time for the same stimulus. The classic example of this is a bathroom scale which reads 180 the first time you step on it, but 173 if you immediately step back on. Your weight has not changed – the measure simply cannot be trusted. Time for a new scale! Similarly, if your employee's performance is about the same from one quarter to the next, but you rate her high the first quarter and lower the second quarter, there is a question. This question is, "What changed?" – for it was not her performance. In this case, the rating cannot be trusted just like the scale's reading could not be trusted. It is unreliable.

Contaminated measures include irrelevant information in addition to relevant. For example, if you as manager were to judge employees' performance on the degree of friendliness they show, that would be criterion contamination, assuming that friendliness toward you does not impact job performance. (Incidentally, supervisors' liking of subordinates does seem to affect ratings, as researchers Joel Lefkowitz and Mariangela Battista found. While understandable, managers in most cases should try to limit this effect.)

Job performance measures can also be described as *deficient*, if they fail to include important job performance information. An example might be: you are assessing overall job performance in order to rank employees in promotion potential, but fail to include a critical dimension such as "acts as a team player." Leaving that out is a kind of lack, or deficiency, in the assessment.

A measure is called *biased* if it is systematically sloped higher or lower in response to some irrelevant characteristic, such as gender. This can also be seen as a kind of criterion contamination (gender is extraneous). Or, a measure can be biased in that it is usually too high, or too low, than is warranted by reality. An example of the latter would be if workers' outputs are regularly under- or overcounted by some tracking system.

These problems – unreliability, contamination, deficiency, and bias – are common problems that plague performance measurement. In the search for reliable, valid assessment they are encountered all the time. Being aware of the high probability of their appearance is already some defense, in that management can see them and take them into account.

To the measurement challenges of reliability, contamination, deficiency and bias, add the point that Max Planck was making in the quote at the beginning of this chapter. Planck was maintaining that as soon as you measure, you change the phenomenon you are looking at. There is even a sense into which you bring that phenomenon into being.

Planck derived this insight at least in part through his work in quantum mechanics. But his statement applies to the macro world, and even the world of bricks.

Consider the production of bricks under two conditions. The first is: you and some friends decide that having some bricks would be useful – in order to build a shed, say. Then you all go about producing some bricks (after watching a YouTube video on how to do this). There is no particular production schedule, and you discover some interesting aspects of this task as you carry out the whole project. You have enjoyable conversations throughout, and your friendships deepen.

The second condition is like the first, except one of your friends suggests that 100 bricks need to be produced each day. This, he says, will mean the shed will be done in time for winter. This seems logical and you all agree. The number of completed bricks will be counted each hour of each day in order to assure that everything is on track. Work can stop for the day when the requisite number of bricks are produced.

By putting in place this target, measurement has become a "taskmaster." The target means there must be a schedule of work. To meet this schedule, you find that times for meals and rest need to be regulated. Perhaps one of your friends, irritated by needing to make quota, questions the need of a shed at all. Or perhaps she decides to game the system and begins to make smaller or more fragile bricks in order to complete the workday earlier. This results in heated disagreements, and perhaps the most outgoing, energetic person decides they should be the "boss."

The Book of Exodus refers to "taskmasters" who required workers to produce a certain number of bricks – that is, the number of bricks produced was counted. Thus there is an inevitable result of setting a target; measurement creates a human representative of itself – a living taskmaster.

You may point out that in the first condition, the job of producing bricks didn't rise above that of a hobby – the group of friends were doing it for fun, so to speak. The eventual shed was a "nice to have." In the second condition, actual work emerges: a brick production target was determined (one might say, arose) since the goal of having the shed completed before winter seemed like a very reasonable idea. If you feel the first condition is hobby-like, I think this is correct. It is in serious (that is, non-hobby like) enterprises that it is natural for both measurement and management to appear.

Of course, management does not necessarily mean taskmasterhood. The word taskmaster is a harsh word, perhaps not relevant for many managers today. It implies *driving* workers more than *leading* them.

Nonetheless, creating and implementing metrics will often have many negative effects. We'll continue to discuss this in the following chapters.

Max Karl Ernst Ludwig Planck (1858-1947) was a theoretical physicist, known especially for his work in quantum theory. He developed a mathematical constant, h, which is central to many values calculated for the subatomic level of reality. Like many theoretical physicists, he saw that the act of observation was somehow connected to the nature of the reality observed.

Lefkowitz, J., & Battista, M. (1995). Potential sources of criterion bias in supervisor ratings used for test validation. *Journal of Business and Psychology*, *9*, 389-414.

Planck, M. (2017). *Where is science going?* Pickle Partners Publishing.

Stern, A. (1956). Science and the philosopher. *American Scientist, 44(3)*, 281-295.

15. Performance Management II: The Lasting Insights of St. Deming

Quality Control guru Deming may not actually be a saint, but he was almost mystically profound when it came to Performance Management

Merit ratings leave "people bitter, crushed, bruised, battered, desolate, despondent, dejected, feeling inferior, some even depressed, unfit for work for weeks after receipt of rating." – William Edwards Deming

William Deming is, of course, not officially a saint nor a mystic (though his premises might seem mystical to some schools of management). Deming was a pioneer, a foundational figure, in the Quality Control movement. Much of what he said has been taken to heart by corporate leadership, and it is without doubt true that the quality (lack of defects) and hence durability of many common products is now much higher than previously.

Nonetheless, at least one aspect of his preaching has failed to take hold in business. You may have come across his "Seven Sins of Western Management," but as a refresher, here they are:

1. Lack of constancy of purpose

2. Emphasis on short-term profits. (Overreaction to short term variation is harmful to long term success. With such focus on relatively unimportant short-term results focus on constancy of purpose is next to impossible)

3. Evaluation of performance, merit rating or annual review

4. Mobility of top management (too much turnover causes numerous problems)

5. Running a company on visible figures alone (many important factors are "unknown and unknowable")

6. Excessive medical costs

7. Excessive legal damage awards swelled by lawyers working on contingency fees

Although all of these are interesting, I'll focus only on sin #3: *Evaluation of performance, merit rating or annual review*. This is one area in which Deming's teaching has not had much impact.

Evaluation of performance now falls under the umbrella term of Performance Management. Performance Management includes performance goal setting, feedback, rating, ranking, and reviews (reviews, by the way, often occur much more frequently than just annually).

The big picture recognized and articulated by Deming was simple. Quality control demands that we understand not individual behaviors so much as the processes that contain them. This is because, Deming said, 95 percent of problems are traceable to the system and variations in the system, not the individuals within that system.

In fact, focusing on individuals (i.e., trying to increase their engagement, say) represents a "low-yield strategy," according to Deming. If managers look primarily at individuals, they will inevitably see individuals as somehow causing problems that are in actuality mainly due to systems.

The archetypal tool of the quality control movement is the control chart. Characteristics of a product (weight, defects, dimensions, flexibility, durability, etc.) are measured over time and plotted. Acceptable products lie with high and low control lines. Products with characteristics outside the control lines indicate unacceptable variation.

Deming recommended abolishing what we today call Performance Management. But, if individual performance for some reason absolutely *must* be assessed, he didn't hesitate to recommend control charts for this purpose. Here is a hypothetical QC plot for individual performance for call representatives where the minimum acceptable number of calls per day is eight:

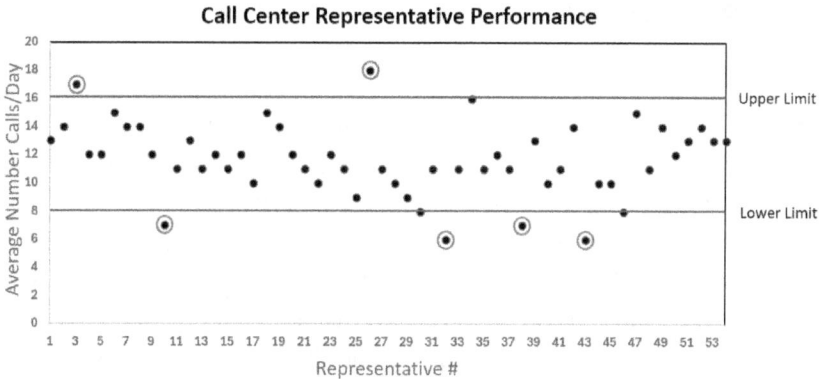

Call Center Representative Performance

If you must measure individual performance, Deming would say, focus only on that performance which is *outside the limits of acceptable variation*. In this case, being above the high control line is actually OK – it represents extraordinary performance. Using this approach, low performers (below the lower control line) might be studied to try to understand what obstacles they are encountering that keep them from completing at least eight calls a day. Super performers (in the chart above, those exceeding twice the minimum acceptable level) might be examined to determine if they have discovered some system improvements that might be captured, for the benefit of all. These super performers might also be rewarded to ensure retention.

Those in the middle range need not be managed directly – in terms of their performance – at all. The urge to make distinctions among them is a mistake. True, the upper and lower limit lines of performance can be moved (narrowed or expanded) if appropriate. This is not managing employees, however, but adjusting requirements of the QC system, making it stricter or more lenient.

But all in all, Deming would prefer we don't measure individual performance at all. As his words at the beginning of the chapter argue, it makes people miserable. Management theorist and advocate of Deming's teachings Peter Scholes explains why: Performance Management is a "who-based" approach to tackling system-based problems in the workplace.

In an earlier chapter, we saw that attention has been likened to a searchlight, which illuminates and separates out a narrow range of reality. We cannot help but look where the light is. (This is somewhat reminiscent of the inebriated man who searched for his car keys under the streetlamp, "Because that is where the light is"). The most important aspects of the world, however, may lie outside of the lit area. If our spotlight is on the "who," say Scholes and Deming, we miss the system. In fact, one is likely to "go down a rabbit hole," looking at variables like motivation and engagement. But if we focus on the system, we can track variation in products and outcomes and work to *identify the sources of variation*. Reduce, fix, or minimize those sources, and you improve quality automatically. And, incidentally but importantly, you are less likely to reduce motivation and engagement through excessive examination of people!

In short, the goal should be to control processes, not employees.

Deming was (probably) not a true mystic, but he *was* a guru who had a unique perspective on PM that might be mystical, for all the understanding it seems to garner. And this perspective – a relentless focus on the performance of the system, not individual employees – perhaps can give managers freedom. They can be more free than is typical, maybe, to see employees as persons rather than as means. And, as true mystic Martin Buber once observed, "When we encounter another individual truly as a person, not as an object for use, we become fully human." If managers allow employees to be true persons and encounter them in that way, they have a chance to be true persons themselves.

It might be odd to think that managers are prevented from being truly and fully human because of a Performance Management system that examines individual performance rather than the system within which those individuals labor. However, there is no doubt that Performance Management is disliked – intensely – by both managers and employees. Maybe its odd but real estranging and dehumanizing effect is one reason why.

William Edwards Deming (1900-1993) was a statistician and engineer. He interned at Western Electric's Hawthorne Works, home of the famous Hawthorne studies. Deming helped the US Census to develop sampling procedures before WWII and was a census consultant to the Japanese government under the MacArthur administration of that country. He taught Japanese engineers/manufacturers statistical process control and brought these teachings back to the United States.

Deming, W. E. (2018). *Out of the crisis*, reissue. MIT press.

Scholtes, P. R. (1993). Total quality or performance appraisal: choose one. *National Productivity Review*, 12(3), 349-363.

Buber, M. (1970). *I and Thou* (Vol. 243). Simon and Schuster.

16. Performance Management III: Managers and Employee Surveillance

A parable by Franz Kafka reminds us of the dangers of surveilling our employees

> "I ran past the first watchman. Then I was horrified, ran back again and said to the watchman: 'I ran through here while you were looking the other way.' The watchman gazed ahead of him and said nothing. 'I suppose I really oughtn't to have done it,' I said. The watchman still said nothing. 'Does your silence indicate permission to pass?'" – Franz Kafka

One of the most treacherous developments of workplace technology is the ability to track employee performance surreptitiously. There is a plethora of ways that managers can leverage such developments to look at what their employees are doing or have done. In some cases, surveillance abilities could be extensive enough to give renewed relevance to an old and discarded word for boss: "overseer."

Part of the problem is the question of what to measure. As mentioned in other chapters, direction and guidance is one of management's central roles. So the examination of performance is normal, and seems necessary for reaching decisions on such things as promotion, training, and rewards. It can be excessive, though, and as Quality Control expert Deming pointed out, Performance Management can be destructive of motivation and morale. In fact, it often is. This conundrum – that measuring performance both is necessary and experienced as bad, cannot be easily solved.

But overall, we exist within the conundrum – damned if we do, damned if we don't. Many researchers currently – and, in my perception, reluctantly – have accepted the debilitating nature of merit rating and performance reviews, but have no solution on offer except ideas such as managing to employee strengths rather than weaknesses, making feedback to employees "future-oriented," setting goals collaboratively, focusing on teams rather than individuals, and so forth.

In any case, it is true that employee surveillance can have negative consequences, some of which are less known than others. For example, consider the fact that surveillance and monitoring is associated with job level, and hence status. The higher one is in the hierarchy, the less one's performance is examined closely. This is in part due to the fact that higher jobs tend to have more discretion – there are more and even unpredictable ways to accomplish tasks. This means that, for such jobs, it is unlikely for simple metrics to capture job performance in any useful way. Of course, this oddly "hidden" privilege of high-discretion jobs means that there is more chance for abuse. And every once in a while, some astonishing dereliction of duties of someone in these higher echelons comes out.

One robust finding is that this gradient of autonomy from low to high corresponds to health and life expectancy. Researcher in epidemiology and public health Michael Marmot clearly showed this in his book *The Status Syndrome*. Due largely, he suspects, to lower job autonomy, workers who have less status have more health problems and live less long than those with higher status. And, one of the key aspects of employee monitoring is the message it sends on job holders' status: the more monitoring, the less status.

But there are other negative aspects of employee surveillance. American psychologist Lloyd Strickland found that surveillance of employees causes an odd problem for managers. Specifically, managers feel less trust toward those employees who are monitored. This is because employees have never had an opportunity to demonstrate that they can work on their own, that they can show initiative and judgement. Surveillance, ironically, thus acts as a barrier to obtaining useful information about employees. In addition, Strickland showed that managers express a greater need to monitor workers who are already being monitored. Managers face a "self-perpetuating information loss": they don't trust monitored employees, and they feel a continuing need to monitor exactly those employees.

If monitoring can prevent the development of the trust that managers need to have in their employees, it can of course also damage the trust and performance of employees. Cognitive Evaluation Theory predicts that the surveilled employee, if they sense that this monitoring is designed for control, will develop an external "locus of control." Their motivation will tend to be extrinsic (that is, relying on rewards and external conditions) rather than intrinsic (driven by meaning). This affects product quality in a negative way; quantity less so.

Kafka's parable at the top of the chapter highlights another, and rarely imagined, negative effect of performance monitoring. He pictures a person who recognizes that monitoring capabilities (represented by the watchman) exist. And it seems that the very existence of such capabilities causes the person to believe she *should be monitored*. The watchman in the parable doesn't point out or seem to note the person's activities. The subject is disturbed by this and seems to want to make up for this shortfall. In effect, she interiorizes the monitoring and reports her own activities, of her own volition.

Whether monitoring can reduce people to being their own surveillant in the workplace is unresearched. But given what we know about human psychology, it is certainly conceivable. (Consider, for example, the Stockholm Syndrome, where a person begins to identify with their own abductors).

Autonomy at work can be damaged by surveillance. Kafka offers a dark extension of this. He suggests that surveillance can attack people directly. In response to it, they may proactively diminish their own autonomy (and hence sense of meaning and purpose), by becoming their own watchers.

Franz Kafka (1883-1924) was born and lived in Prague (which was part of the Austro-Hungarian Empire, Czechoslovakia after 1918). His personality has been described as schizoid and he thought himself ugly, but he was considered handsome and possessing a sense of humor by his friends. He wrote the important novels *The Trial* and *The Castle* as well as numerous short works.

Note: An earlier discussion of this parable of Kafka by the author appeared in *Psyche* (reference below).

Alliger, G.M. (2022). Kafka warned us: surveillance turns the watched into watchers. *Psyche*, December.

Kafka, F. (1961). *Parables and paradoxes*. Schocken.

Marmot, M. (2005). *Status syndrome: How your social standing directly affects your health*. A&C Black.

Strickland, L. H. (1958). Surveillance and trust. *Journal of Personality*. *26,* 200–215.

17. Performance Management IV: Right Rewards

Zen master Sozan thinks counterintuitively about how to reward work

> "Is it better to give the builder three cash, or better to give him two cash, or better to give him one cash?" asked Sozan.

Sozan was a Chinese Zen master, one of the founders of the Soto ("Silent Illumination" school). In the quote above, he is asking a monk how much a contractor should be paid. Because of its odd beauty, the whole passage is reproduced below (Note that "Zenji" and "Oshō" are monastic titles of rank, and "cash" is an archaic unit of currency).

Sozan's Memorial Tower

Once, when the monk who was director of affairs in the monastery came to Sozan Nin Zenji about the construction of the Master's memorial tower, the Zenji said: "How much money will you give the builder?"

"That rests with you, Oshō."

"Is it better to give the builder three cash, or better to give him two cash, or better to give him one cash?" asked Sozan. "However, if you can speak build the tower for me yourself."

The monk was dumbfounded.

At that time Rasan was living in a hermitage on the Daiyu Peak. One day a monk who came to the mountain to see him recounted this conversation between Sozan and the director of affairs at the monastery.

"Has anyone been able to speak?" asked Rasan.

"As yet, no one, replied the monk."

"Then go back to Sozan, said Rasan, and tell him this: if you give the builder one cash, you won't get a memorial tower in your entire lifetime; if you give him two cash you and he together will be a single hand; if you give him three cash, you will do him such injury that his eyebrows and hair will fall out."

The monk returned and gave the message to Sozan. The Zenji assumed a dignified manner and, gazing far off toward the Daiyu Peak, bowed and said: "I had thought there was no man who could speak, but on the Daiyu Peak is an old Buddha who emits dazzling shafts of light reaching even to this distance."

I reviewed this *koan* in a previous book. There the discussion centered around how much to pay contractors that you might hire at home, for a given job. In sum, I think the story of the memorial tower suggests that you can pay him or her too much ("three cash"), too little ("one cash"), or the right amount ("two cash").

But let's look at rewards in the workplace, where you may have contractors and/or full-time employees. Managers have a number of reward levers they can pull: bonuses, promotions, recognition, and perks of various kinds. We won't go into detail on these, since the particular rewards over which any manager has control will differ greatly from organization to organization.

What seems unique in the story of Sozan is the idea you can reward someone too much. It's easy and perhaps fairly common to offer someone too little. What managers should want to do is offer the proper level of reward. But Sozan says you can overshoot, doing "such injury" that "eyebrows and hair will fall out." How and why, exactly, would things work in that way?

First, research in work psychology does suggest that, under some specific conditions, overpayment can reduce worker motivation. It seems to operate in this way: if a worker begins to be paid more than is sensible even for very good performance, she may interpret her own reasons for working differently than if she is paid what she deems appropriate. Her understanding of why she is working hard begins to focus on the extrinsic, rather than the intrinsic, nature of the job. Previously, she may have considered that it was her interest in the job that kept her attentive and focused. Now, she feels that she does the work in a purely transactional sense: to receive the money. The payment has become so salient that it undermines her engagement in the job itself alone.

Sozan's story lends itself to a second, though related, interpretation. Perhaps ironically, too much reward could make an employee think twice about how much management values her precisely as a person. With the current increasing emphasis on appreciating the worker as a person and not just a producer, too much reward could suggest an off-hand, distant attitude on the part of the company. Money may be there but recognition lacking. At the very least, then, it will be important to recognize employees – not just pay them well. Good recognition should be made in front of, or otherwise include, peers and teammates.

Third, excessive reward could act to isolate an employee unless management communicates that it understands and appreciates not just the worker herself, but her job. Managers should stay close enough to the actual work being conducted to be able to discuss that work intelligently and well with employees. If you are made a manager over employees whose jobs you do not understand… make it your job to understand their jobs. Otherwise you will inevitably be "out of touch" and unable to engage in those content-rich conversations that will be gratifying, rewarding, to employees.

Sozan's concept of the right level of reward is an uncommon one. But a few minutes wondering whether and how it might apply to your own management can't hurt.

Sozan (837-909) was a founder of Soto, or "quiet" school, Zen; he was popularly known as Uncle Dwarf.

Miura, I. & Fuller Sasaki, R. (1965). *The Zen koan: Its history and use in Rinzai Zen*. San Diego: Harcourt Brace Jovanovich.

18. Performance Management V: Effort versus Results

Two thinkers, one Islamic, one Hindu, take an approach to work that suggests a managerial change of perspective re Performance Management

"Indeed, Allah loves one who when he does a work, he does it with *itqan* [strives for perfection]." – Al-Bayhaqi

"Satisfaction lies in the effort, not in the attainment. Full effort is full victory." – Mohandas Gandhi

If you search for discussions of the value of effort separate from the results of that effort, you find very little. Mostly what turns up are thoughts on how one will never get results without effort. It's motivational: work hard and you will succeed!

The link between effort and results can't be denied, in this sense: with no effort you'll get no results. But you may also expend great effort and get no results. It's like this:

	No Results	Results
Effort	✓	✓
No Effort	✓	

The simple takeaway might be: whatever you do, put in effort. That way you'll have a chance to succeed at what you are trying to do.

However, I'd like to focus on the rarely thought-about outcome represented by the upper-left checkmark, which indicates that effort does not necessarily result in success.

Do you, as a manager, reward employees for effort regardless of outcomes, regardless of their "success" in having achieved the specific goals that you and they have agreed on? You may say, "No, as a manager it is precisely their performance (that is, results) that I am tasked to reward. Effort without reward is not really what we are shooting for." And that makes sense. If one of your salespersons apparently tries hard but is continually under quota, then of what good to you and the company is the effort he expended? The same with any job, whether service, production, or other. It's the results that count in the end.

But, as we know, not all outcomes are under our employees' control. In fact, look back at Deming's arguments in Chapter 14. His central point is that the influence of the system, by and large, dwarfs individual effort when it comes to outcomes. If there is a problem with results, fix the system.

This cannot mean that effort is unimportant. In fact, I want to argue that it is important in its own right, aside from results, outcomes, and success.

First, as a manager you ought to recognize employee effort separately from the outcomes of that effort. By doing so you are helping them to see themselves as people who may not always succeed, but who are worthy of attention and respect nonetheless. And who always succeeds? Who has not put days or weeks into a project only to see it fail or fall short for one reason or another?

Second, consider the research results carefully detailed by Michael Marmot in *The Status Syndrome*. Some employees in his database were identified as people who believed that even though they had worked hard in a job, they were not recognized (through rewards such as compensation, promotion, respect). These employees had a much higher risk of coronary disease than others who believed that they were appropriately recognized. This suggests perhaps that valuing employee effort – giving them status – even separate from results, far from being unimportant, is a critical managerial strategy – at least, if we care about the long-term health of our workers.

Finally, there is the curious character of effort in and of itself. It changes how we perceive the value of the outcome that is finally achieved. Specifically, a phenomenon called the *effort paradox* exists. This is the paradox: that we may well value something more if we exerted more effort to accomplish or acquire it. And the reason this is paradoxical is that it contravenes the common idea that effort is a cost that does not add value.

Moreover, effort can become rewarding in and of itself. The idea of "learned industriousness" (developed initially in animal studies) explains how this is so. Over time, if high effort does result in high reward, an association develops such that expending effort becomes a "secondary reinforcer." In this case, the perceived value of effort may generalize, such that when a new task is presented it will be tackled with a verve missing among those in a control group.

Given the above, it seems to me that it makes sense to reward effort. To do so makes it more likely that employees will be healthier and will persevere even in the face of lack of success. This perseverance is a type of resilience.

Not mentioned yet is the "fail fast" management approach. If employees are inculcated with this idea, initial lack of success across even many trials will not damage their motivation. Instead, they will work within the spirit that the road to eventual success is expected to be littered with failures. True, "fail fast" is typically limited to engineering-like production, but it seems likely that it could be extended to other work domains. How does a salesperson maintain zeal when encountering failures in her cold calling? By honing her technique, and valuing the effort itself that she is putting in.

Noor Liza Adnan and colleagues have proposed an Islamic approach to Performance Management. Key to this proposal is the concept that outcomes, which are determined by Allah, are not necessarily immediate, regardless of effort. Desired results *may* come immediately, or they may be stored up for the future, or an evil of similar magnitude may be averted. And, as in the quote at the top of the page, Allah loves the effort itself. For this reason, it is simply *fairer* to recognize effort in addition to outcomes. The result will be a happier and more mentally balanced workforce.

Mohandas Gandhi sums it up starkly: "Satisfaction lies in the effort, not in the attainment. Full effort is full victory." Can we bring ourselves to believe that? In this very real world, it might help us, and our employees, if we could at least ponder this apparently unworldly message.

Al-Bayhaqi (994–1066) was a famed Sunni ascetic, scholar, and author. The quote above appears in Shu'ab al-Iman ("The Branches of Faith").

Mohandas Karamchand Gandhi (1869-1948) was an advocate of non-violence and a prominent political player in the move toward an independent India. He was assassinated by a nationalist opposed to Gandhi's non-violent teachings, which he felt disadvantaged Hindus.

Adnan, N. L., Wan Jusoh, W. N. H., Muda, R., & Yusoff, R. (2021). A proposed Islamic performance management model (IPMM): Towards more productive employees with better quality of work life. *Advances in Business Research International Journal*, 7(2), 145-160.

Gandhi, M. (1922). *Young India*, Sept. 3.

Inzlicht, M., Shenhav, A., & Olivola, C. Y. (2018). The effort paradox: Effort is both costly and valued. *Trends In Cognitive Sciences*, *22(4)*, 337-349.

Marmot, M. (2005). *Status syndrome: How your social standing directly affects your health*. A&C Black.

19. Moving On: Avoiding Rumination at Work

A story of two monks shows how rumination on past actions ought to be avoided

Two monks were walking through the village and came upon a woman standing on a wooden sidewalk. She wanted to cross the street to the other side but didn't wish to get muddy. The older monk helped her across, picking her up and carrying her to the other side. Much later, as the two monks walked on, the younger one suddenly started to berate the older for carrying the woman, for as monks they were prohibited contact with the opposite sex. The older monk responded, "Are you still carrying that woman?" – Zen tale

This popular Zen story is sometimes told with a river in place of the street. In any case, unlike some Zen *koans*, this one has a simple (though profound) take-away message – mental freedom is found in the lack of restlessly worrying or fretting about something. We can call this kind of worry "rumination." Some individuals may indeed never ruminate, but most do at times, and some often.

Rumination on the past, on the present, or the future is, in fact, a kind of psychological "own goal." That is, it is a seemingly unnecessary personal movement into dark places. It can drain one's energy and dampen one's mood. Research consistently shows rumination to be correlated with depression, anxiety, demoralization, self-doubt, and even somatic complaints. And it can affect not only mood, but every kind of performance, including manager and employee job performance. The effects on performance – such as problem solving or developing and maintaining social relationships – are probably due to "captured" mental capacity that would otherwise be available for constructive activities.

Researcher Jay Brinker and colleagues define rumination as "a stable style of thinking marked by repetitive, recurrent, intrusive and uncontrollable thoughts." Two negative characteristics of rumination show clearly in that definition. First, the thoughts that are typical of rumination are intrusive – that is, not desired. Ruminative thoughts may repeatedly circle back to negative nodes, such as, "I'm such a loser," "why don't I feel like getting anything done?" "I wish I could just disappear," "how could I have been so stupid?" "no one here really likes me." Second, rumination is a kind of bondage – it seems to be not only "intrusive" but "uncontrollable."

"Ruminate" *can* have neutral or even positive meanings, as when one is pleasurably "ruminating on a problem" – in this case, the word is a synonym for "ponder." But, in the sense we are using it here, rumination is essentially a repetitive focusing on some apparently negative circumstances and on one's own feelings of depression or sadness.

"Worry" is similar to rumination. However, it is the constant, repetitive, unproductive, "sticky" nature of worrying thoughts, along with sad mood, that signifies rumination.

Those who find themselves ruminating at and/or about work often hope that this thinking will help solve their perceived problems – and provide an end to their ruminating. But rumination does not seem to be helpful in that regard. Instead, it captures mental capacity and depletes emotional resources.

This depletion is an important cause of bad management. Alyson Byrne and her co-researchers recruited and studied almost 200 leader-direct report pairs. In an article that reported their results, the authors point out that when personal resources run low, leaders (including managers) are less likely to engage in the positive behaviors of "transformational leadership" and more likely to display abusive supervision. Here, transformational leadership involves being a good role model, communicating overarching and inspiring goals, challenging reports to solve problems creatively, and recognizing and providing appropriate consideration to employees. Abusive supervision includes verbal and non-verbal (but not physical) hostility – being rude, dismissive, or disrespectful. To the extent, then, that rumination by managers depletes their mental, emotional, and physical reserves, it can undermine their management effectiveness and even lead to actively bad management.

Other work researchers have studied how work-related rumination is a barrier to recovery from work. Specifically, if persistent work-related worrying spills over into non-work life, a downward cycle of ever-greater mental and physical depletion may be initiated. The result in this case could be burnout.

There is good news, however. This is that rumination may be, if not completely avoided as in the case of the older monk in the story, at least reduced and contained. Suppression of negative thoughts does not seem to work. One suggestion is instead to focus on positive thoughts or to distract oneself with some pleasant activity. In a sense, the idea is to replace one's negative thinking with more positive thinking. Many other therapeutic approaches exist for serious cases of rumination, such as those found in individuals with diagnoses of OCD or PTSD.

But for non-pathological cases of rumination, making a decision to simply think on different and more pleasant topics may be enough. In my experience, one possible avenue for doing this, and which is nowhere discussed in the research literature, is trust.

The role of trust in overcoming rumination would work like this. Much rumination occurs because of a persistent set of worries about how another person is going to react or is reacting to some action of one's own. For example, suppose you send an important email. You expect a quick reply, but none is forthcoming. Over time, perhaps just a few hours, you begin to worry. Could you somehow, perhaps through awkward wording, have offended the recipient? Soon you can't stop thinking about it, going round and round in your mind with examinations and explanations, hopes and fears.

But consider: you sent the email in good faith; you have not known the recipient to go ballistic previously over small details; there may be many reasons for a slow response; *and* ruminating is doing no good (unless indeed it convinces you to send a clarifying note – which, however, could just heighten your concerns if again the response is delayed). One way to cease ruminating is simply to *trust the other person* to respond, in time, in a rational, respectful way. I believe that consciously making an action of trust, as it were, in this way is a decision we can make. It might require some discipline, but it can get you out of the dank basement of rumination.

It is almost a case of minding one's own business. You wrote the email. The expected response is their business, not yours. In the case of the young monk of the story, he might – instead of building up a head of steam via rumination on the older monk's seeming transgression – have simply trusted that any infraction would be handled interiorly by the other. Presumably, he knew him to be a good monk. So, the younger monk might have minded his own business, and worked on the inner freedom such monks are supposed to cultivate.

A final word can be provided by William Blake, who eloquently says that really, we shouldn't hold too tightly onto even pleasant things – never mind disturbing things. That is because:

> He who binds to himself a joy
>
> Does the wingèd life destroy;
>
> He who kisses the joy as it flies
>
> Lives in eternity's sunrise.

The story of the two monks (Tanzan and Ekido) is possibly apocryphal. I have adapted it here from the book *Zen Flesh Zen Bones*.

Brinker, J. K., & Dozois, D. J. (2009). Ruminative thought style and depressed mood. *Journal of Clinical Psychology*, *65*(1), 1-19.

Brinker, J. K., Chin, Z. H., & Wilkinson, R. (2014). Ruminative thinking style and the MMPI-2-RF. *Personality and Individual Differences*, *66*, 102-105.

Byrne, A., Dionisi, A.M., Barling, J., Akers, A., Robertson, J., Lys, R., Wylie, J. and Dupré, K. (2014). The depleted leader: The influence of leaders' diminished psychological resources on leadership behaviors. *The Leadership Quarterly 25(2)*, 344-357.

Cropley, M., & Zijlstra, F. R. (2011). Work and rumination. *Handbook of Stress in the Occupations*, *487*(503), 10-4337.

Purdon, C. (2003). *Psychological treatment of rumination*. In Depressive rumination: Nature, Theory and Treatment, 217-239.

Reps, P., & Senzaki, N. (1998). *Zen flesh, Zen bones: A collection of Zen and pre-Zen writings*. Tuttle Publishing.

20. Four Kinds of Psychological Detachment

Mentally detaching at work (and in life) can be bad or it can be good

> "Those who are enjoying life should live as though there were nothing to laugh about; those whose life is buying things should live as though they had nothing of their own; and those who have to deal with the world should not become engrossed in it." – Paul of Tarsus

To "detach," according to Merriam-Webster, means to separate from something larger, "usually without violence or damage." But psychological detachment can occur without, or with, damage. It depends on the type of detachment.

There are three kinds of detachment that psychologists may talk about. Then there is a fourth kind that Paul portrays in the short quote above. Four ways to detach; two of these seem to be good, two bad. It is useful for managers to understand all four.

The first detachment we'll talk about is one of the good ones: *detachment from work when not at work.* This way to detach is conceptualized as the ability to leave the job at work. Specifically, it is defined as the absence of work-related thoughts while not at work. One can visualize a healthy cycle. In the first part of the cycle, a person is immersed in work while in the workplace (wherever that workplace may be, office, road, home). In the next part of the cycle, the person is off work and simply not thinking about it. Return to the immersion of work, then again to being fully not working, and so forth.

Researchers have reviewed the predictors and outcomes of this kind of detachment from work. Successful detaching occurs more frequently for people who are not highly negative in mood, for whom job demands are lower, and who are less heavily invested in their work. Successful detaching from work when not at work is related to various outcomes of reported psychological health, such as lower exhaustion, better sleep, and higher well-being.

One interesting caveat, however, is that not thinking about work when not in the workplace may be related to lower creativity and "contextual job performance" (contextual job performance includes so-called "citizenship" behaviors that show personal initiative and go beyond the tasks in the job description, such as volunteering to assist co-workers). So there may be some advantages to an organization when some employees are absorbed in work all the time, even away from work. Nonetheless, the general benefits to the employee of successfully detaching from work when not in the workplace are clear.

Interestingly, that this kind of detachment from work can be trained was reported by psychologists Tina Karabinski and colleagues. These researchers found that if you train employees in such things as boundary management, emotion regulation, and sleep improvement, you can increase their ability to "leave work at work." Boundary management can be trained by such things as emphasizing the importance of breaks from work and instituting activities such as a positive "ritual" before work begins. Emotional regulation can be increased through teaching employees how to redirect their attention and how to reframe, or reappraise, their situations. Ways to improve the quality of sleep are well-known and varied.

It is important to note that being detached from work when not at work need not limit employees' degree of work *engagement*. Maria Gaudiino and Giovanni De Stefano, for example, found that a substantial subgroup of employees demonstrate both high detachment from work when not at work, and high work engagement when at work.

In sum, the first type of detachment is simply a healthy separation from work – a lack of rumination about work – when not at work. It is associated with good outcomes for both employees and organizations. It can be trained, at least to some extent.

A second type of detachment is bad: *job burnout*. This is an umbrella term; job burnout is characterized by cynicism, emotional and possibly physical exhaustion, and a loss of belief in one's own ability to accomplish work-related goals. Job burnout can be considered a kind of detachment because a burned-out employee fundamentally *cannot* engage fully in her job any longer. The psychological resources to do so have been consumed. Causes of burnout are multiple and differ from job to job and employee to employee. Often, however, there is a basic mismatch between job demands and the resources that an organization supplies to help employees meet those demands. For example, there may not be enough nurses to meet the needs of a hospital, resulting in excess workload. Unfair policies or treatment by management, role ambiguity, job insecurity, and continuous demands to interact socially (e.g., by call center representatives), are other causes of burnout.

Possibly ironically, failure to detach healthily from work while not at work (the first kind of detachment) can lead to burnout, the second and harmful kind of detachment. Managers need to be on the alert for conditions that might foster burnout. The very term "burnout" suggests that it takes time for an employee to reach this negative end point, and also that this endpoint is really very bad and not easily remedied once reached.

There is a third, and much rarer, kind of detachment we can discuss briefly. Like burnout, it is a negative state for any person, employee or not. It is rare because it is clinically pathological. We can term this *dissociative detachment*. In its severest form, dissociation occurs when the "moorings in inner and outer reality" are loosened, as Jon Allen and colleagues point out. This type of detachment shows itself in two basic qualities: being detached from one's own actions, and being detached from one's environment and own self. For example, some people have the experience of not being sure whether things that they remember happening really did happen or whether they just dreamed them. Or they may experience "derealization," where people and things do not seem real, but rather are seen as if through a fog, or even as props or actors on a stage.

Questions assessing this kind of detachment range from what might actually be common experiences (such as: "When listening to someone talk, I suddenly realize I do not hear part or all of what was said") to presumably much less common experiences (for example, "I feel mechanical, like a robot or like I'm not really human").

While managers are unlikely to encounter dissociative detachment often, it's important to remember that some PTSD sufferers may experience dissociation at times. Some kinds of drugs, mental illness, and brain damage can also cause or facilitate dissociative detachment.

So then there are at least three types of detachment, one good and two bad. First, there is the healthy detachment from work when not at work. This is characterized by not being bothered by thoughts of work when not at work. Second, there is burnout, a kind of detachment from work that can occur when high job demands are coupled with insufficient resources and lack of control. Third, there is a clinically pathological kind of detachment characterized by a loss of connection to self.

At this point, let's turn to a fourth kind of detachment. I suggest that it is being *healthily detached from work while at work.*

Consider what Paul says: "Those who are enjoying life should live as though there were nothing to laugh about; those whose life is buying things should live as though they had nothing of their own; and those who have to deal with the world should not become engrossed in it."

Paul here is describing with words something difficult to describe with words. What he is recommending seems to be a stance, an attitude, an orientation towards ourselves and our environment. But one must admit that it is curious – laughing as though there were no reason to laugh, owning without really owning, dealing with the world without engagement. There is no suggestion that one's effectiveness in dealing with the world – for example, when working – is at all hampered or constrained. Rather, one is working as if not working.

It is true that for Paul the current state of the world was under a kind of sentence – it might end in the near future. So it made sense for him to recommend this detached, ready-to-move-on-to-other-things, attitude.

But the "be detached even while active" advice occurs in other cultures besides the one in which Paul lived. A saying that may agree with Paul is attributed to Zen master Hakuin: "Empty handed, yet holding a hoe; walking, yet riding a water buffalo." Non-action within action.

"Working as if not working" – this is the key, if there is one. It seems to be a simple contradiction, one perhaps to be dismissed. But like many of the statements of the mystics, a paradox or contradiction is used to describe a unitary reality.

I wonder whether a manager observing an employee acting along Paul's suggested lines might think: It seems like this person isn't all here today. I hope everything is OK. I wonder the best way to ensure that they are more engaged.

On the other hand, it is possible that an employee of this inclination might not stand out as unengaged at all. She might simply be working from a remarkable inner freedom. She is detached, but in a way that cannot be observed. In that case, she has escaped, and is her own manager.

Paul of Tarsus (St. Paul the Apostle) was born around 0 AD and died around 65 AD. Famously, he was a persecutor of the early Church, experienced conversion, and founded Christian communities. He wrote many letters, some of which are included in the New Testament.

Allen, J. G., Coyne, L., & Console, D. A. (1997). Dissociative detachment relates to psychotic symptoms and personality decompensation. *Comprehensive Psychiatry, 38(6)*, 327-334.

Butler, C., Dorahy, M. J., & Middleton, W. (2019). The Detachment and Compartmentalization Inventory (DCI): An assessment tool for two potentially distinct forms of dissociation. *Journal of Trauma & Dissociation, 20(5)*, 526-547.

Gaudiino, M., & Di Stefano, G. (2023). To detach or not to detach? The role of psychological detachment on the relationship between heavy work investment and well-being: A latent profile analysis. *Current Psychology, 42(8)*, 6667-6681.

Karabinski, T., Haun, V. C., Nübold, A., Wendsche, J., & Wegge, J. (2021). Interventions for improving psychological detachment from work: A meta-analysis. *Journal of Occupational Health Psychology, 26(3)*, 224.

Olsen, S. A., Clapp, J. D., Parra, G. R., & Beck, J. G. (2013). Factor structure of the Dissociative Experiences Scale: An examination across sexual assault status. *Journal of Psychopathology and Behavioral Assessment, 35*, 394-403.

Wendsche, J., & Lohmann-Haislah, A. (2017). A meta-analysis on antecedents and outcomes of detachment from work. *Frontiers in Psychology, 7*, 2072.

21. Leaders vs Managers: Accepting the Role of Manager

The roles are distinctly different

"The ruler stays in the kingdom, the general goes beyond the frontiers." – Zen Master Hongzhi

"Love work; hate lordship; and do not become overly intimate with the ruling powers." – The Sage Shemayah

---

Researchers have long thought about the differences between the roles of leaders and managers (as nicely summarized by Shamas-Ur-Rehman Toor). Most of what Toor and others have perceived is obvious enough: Leadership is about change, vision, inspiration, and the future; management is about the complexities of projects and tasks, methods, guidance, and the present.

But pondering the words, above, of Hongzhi and Shemayah may add some nuance.

Zen Master Hongzhi merely states what seems to be an obvious truth: as a rule, rulers stay back home. And generally, they allow their generals to wage the wars, wars which may take them far afield. There have been times, of course, where rulers themselves fought on the front lines. These are exceptions.

It's easy to see why this should be so: the generals are specialists in warfare. Rulers simply have large goals, such as "repel these attackers," or "take that territory." How that is to be done, the generals usually decide.

Implicit in Hongzhi's observation is that, risky as it may be to be a ruler, generals are at greater risk. They may be "beyond the frontiers," in enemy territory and exposed to enemy fire. In addition, they are close to the action and need to decide how to carry it out with whatever forces and materiel they have. Therefore, they are less insulated from immediate responsibility for immediate outcomes. Managers, it seems to me, share some of this asymmetrical situation.

First, they manage within workforce, technology, and other resource constraints in their attempts to carry out the organization's "vision" (which is decided upon not by them but by leadership). They may face bumpy changes in leadership personalities and vision. They deal daily with employees and perhaps customers, and so are at least on the front lines, if not "beyond the frontiers." Because of their central role, they may be blamed for failures or setbacks that are due to forces and circumstances that are beyond their control.

Second, like generals, managers necessarily need to carry out the strategic vision set out by leadership, whether they agree with it or not. They face pressures to meet metrics set by leadership – metrics which, as we have seen, may create perverse incentives for themselves and workers. This includes incentives to act against one's own best judgement, or even unethically.

Third, I wonder if Hongzhi's generals ever faced meddling by rulers. Did they receive runners into their camps who brought micro-managing messages on how to carry out their wars? For it certainly is the case that managers may be provided, not just with an overarching vision or goal, but also with a surplus of guidance on how they are to manage in order to establish that vision, to meet that goal. It can feel, in fact, like managers are fighting on two fronts: handling leadership meddling on one front, and managing employee efforts on the other. Leaders ought, in fact, to stay in the kingdom and not go beyond the frontiers of their expertise.

Fourth, with all that, generals (and managers) may still be under-rewarded and under-recognized. One of the pitfalls, in the case of generals, is the temptation to wrangle more rewards and attention. McClellan (under Lincoln) and MacArthur (under Roosevelt and then Truman) come to mind in this regard. Managers may be similarly inclined to find ways to rectify the seeming imbalance between their responsibilities and risks, on the one hand, and recognition and rewards on the other. There may be appropriate times for this, but it is easy to value oneself more highly than is ultimately justified.

In the second quote above, the Sage Shemayah was presumably providing advice for everyone when he wrote, "Love work; hate lordship; and do not become overly intimate with the ruling powers." But we can tie this thought also directly to managers. Instead of trying to rectify imbalances in rewards or recognition, Shemayah suggested a three-pronged approach.

First, love work. In the context of our discussion here, this guidance takes the following quality: be heads-down, focused on and even engrossed in your duties. If you do this, little will distract you.

Second, hate lordship – that is, hate lording it over others. Shemaya's advice is couched in the negative, in the sense that a manager should avoid lordship at all costs. In the positive sense, this means trying to enact that "servant leadership" we spoke about earlier.

Finally, Shemaya says "do not become overly intimate with the ruling powers." Do not be fooled into thinking that, if only you could be close to the leadership, it will be better for you. On the contrary, rather than being able to work "heads-down" and execute management in the ways that you know best and that are most natural to you, you may tend to be confused – one foot in the managers' camp and the other in the camp of the leaders.

In one of Jorge Luis Borges' memorable stories, a character realizes "One destiny is no better than another but that every man should revere the destiny he bears within him." Being a leader is not better than being a manager.

And while a manager may not know fully what a leader is up to, according to Shemaya, that's just fine. And, too, leaders – while they "stay in the kingdom" – may fail to appreciate exactly how hard their generals have it "beyond the border." Such is life in an organization.

Master Hongzhi was a famous practitioner and teacher of Chinese Zen, whose life (1091–1157) bridged the Song and Yuan dynasties. He is considered one of the early proponents of the Zen of "Silent Illumination."

Shemaya (Shemaiah, Shmaya; circa first century BCE – first century CE) is reported by the Mishna to have been a convert to Judaism. He attained the status of a Jewish sage, and was a friend of another sage, Abtalion.

Borges, Jorge Luis. (1967). *Biography of Tadeo Isidoro Cruz (1829-74)*. https://www.newyorker.com/magazine/1967/01/07/three-stories

Goldwurm, H. (1982). *History of the Jewish people: the second Temple era*. Mesorah Publications.

Leighton, T. D., & Wu, Y. (2000). *Cultivating the empty field: The silent illumination of Zen master Hongzhi*. Tuttle Publishing.

Toor, S. U. R. (2011). Differentiating leadership from management: An empirical investigation of leaders and managers. *Leadership and Management in Engineering, 11*(4), 310-320.

22. Help but Perhaps not Self Help

Self-reliance has its limits

> Then he asked him, "What is your name?" He replied, "My name is Legion, for there are many of us." – St. Mark

A Roman Legion had 6000 men. So when the man told Jesus his name was Legion, it signified that he was not just possessed but possessed many times over. The quote above is in the gospel of St. Mark, but the story of the Gadarene demoniac also appears in Luke and Matthew.

In today's society, including the workplace, we too are subjected to many and conflicting voices. This chapter is a brief meditation on what they are saying to us.

Many years ago, after a lengthy personal boycott of the news, I began reading the Wall Street Journal. My first impression lingers: "Hmm…," I thought, "There's a poverty of ideas!" This phrase, "poverty of ideas," is one of those delightful psychiatric idioms such as "autochthonous delusion" (a mistaken belief for which no cause is apparent), "perseveration" (continuing to respond to a stimulus now absent), and – of course – any number of syndromes such as the "Alice in Wonderland" syndrome, the "Rabbit" syndrome, and the "Fregoli syndrome" (this last occurring when different people are assumed to be the same person in different guises). But a patient evinces "poverty of ideas" (or "poverty of content") when they speak, perhaps volubly, without really saying much at all. This is not a nonsensical concatenation of words – that phenomenon goes by the more well-known "word salad" – but rather "speech which is general or full of mundane or meaningless recurrences or stereotyped statements." This, for me, was the WSJ – there I could read an article bristling with terms like GDP, GNP, APR, APY, bear, bull, cycles, busts, commodities, and even Black-Scholes (this latter not, I think, to be confused with black holes). Reading such pieces felt like being subjected to a sales pitch by a window or siding contractor – one ends up somehow feeling cognitively impoverished, simultaneously overwhelmed and under-informed.

I've grown used to this reaction of mine to the WSJ. But if the Wall Street Journal can be confusing, it is true that the press in general seems to generate not necessarily poverty of content but something that nonetheless is, when taken as a whole, very odd. Odd and perhaps at odds with mental health.

Consider that the central payload conveyed to me, a private citizen, by the press is that there is something going on I need to be worried about. Or rather many things about which I should worry. Our climate, disease, our politics, our technology, race, an aging population, the economic divide, college students, the arts – you name it. Day after day, it is explained, the world is replete with worrisome issues.

It might be just me, but this florescence of agitating articles appears not just unhealthy but to have a single taproot, which pulls from some vast ever-replenished reservoir of profound unease. True, there are apparently cheerful articles, for example about somewhat-stressed-but-still-bubbly couples who are searching for a livable residence but only have, say, $700,000 at hand for the task. I say apparently cheerful because for most of us that kind of down payment could be on the far side of the moon as far as its accessibility, and maybe that's our fault. Good for them, though, of course.

I doubt, actually, that editors and journalists can help themselves. It's as if they are possessed by an anxiety that seeks to replicate. And, reading and pondering end-of-the-country, end-of-the-world journalism on topic after topic can cause not just a bloodstream full of corticosteroids pushing us into eternal but useless vigilance, but despair and perhaps even self-hate. In fact, maybe reading the news is a penitential act of self-laceration, because we now have nothing else to do but concentrate, complicitly, on symptoms of the End Times.

Presumably aware that it is actively depressing its readers, the press attempts counteraction via a plethora of self-helpy pieces. You can't miss these: tips, hints, and helpful guidance on how to sleep, the best exercises for back pain, how to travel for health, how to raise your teens, where to find Narcan, how best to argue with your significant other. When I pointed this out to a friend, he said "Of course, it sells!" And maybe that is all it is: canny copy to get those eyeballs (speaking of which, you can search for the NYT's timely "What to Know About Bacteria and Eye Drops"). But I'm not convinced that all the self-help advice is only to get/retain subscribers; I suspect these articles are also therapeutic ballast, an (in my opinion unsuccessful) attempt to offset news-induced anxiety.

In the workplace, too, we are confronted with many and conflicting voices. Here also there is a kind of divided messaging. First, there is the "work hard and be productive, be engaged, be loyal, be committed" message. This can stress workers, particularly if managers are indifferent or even blind to employee problems. Indeed, the American Institute of Stress reports that a large majority of US employees suffer from work-related stress, and a quarter say that their jobs are the number one stressor in their lives.

But similar to what we see in the press, there is a second kind of messaging in the workplace, a therapeutic counterpoint. Practice mindfulness, do yoga, use the company-provided ping pong table. When necessary, take time for yourself. Almost all employees report some availability of mental health resources at work. Unfortunately, less than twenty percent of workers actually feel supported by these resources.

You may point out, rightly, that regardless of the societal and workplace voices, neither readers of the news nor employees in the workplace are running about, denuded of self-respect, gashing their wrists, and yelling hopelessly at the sky. Still, anxiety and depression are at remarkably high levels and what voices we listen to makes a difference. Along that line, there is a before-and-after story from a famous source that comes to mind.

As mentioned, Matthew, Mark, and Luke, with minor variations, all relate the story of the demoniac of Gadarene. This man the people of the local town find impossible to restrain. He haunts the local cemetery, and actually is naked, yelling, and gashing himself with rocks. When Jesus arrives in the locality, the agitating demons possessing the man are themselves agitated, and ask – since they know they can't escape being cast from their home – for permission to enter a nearby herd of swine. The demons make this request presumably unaware that the pigs are no more be able to accept them docilely than could the man; the herd immediately immolates itself by drowning.

For the Gadarene, the world is now utterly changed. The townspeople come out to find him not rushing about naked and in ultimate despair, but "seated, clothed, and in his right mind." Frightened by the whole event, the townspeople beg Jesus to leave them.

For me, pure placidity is evoked by the words "seated, clothed, and in his right mind." I feel that I would not want to be a demoniac, but I do want the wholeness of sitting, being comfortably clothed, and – above all – in *my right mind.*

It is interesting, this move from agitation, self-harm, and despair to peace – to our *right* mind, our *normal* inheritance.

HR (or in the larger world, the press) may attempt, via self-help guides and resources, to cure some of the interior disturbances to which they themselves contribute. But the very content-rich story of the Gadarene demoniac seems to propose that, real help though there may be, it is unlikely to be *self*-help.

St. Mark, or Mark the Evangelist, is the author of one of the four gospels in the New Testament. He may have been a Hellenized Jew, who gathered the content for his book from the sermons of St. Peter.

https://www.nytimes.com/2023/04/03/health/eye-drops-explainer.html

New Catholic Bible. (2015). Mark, Chapter 5. Catholic Book Publishing Corp.

"Poverty of Ideas," in *PsychologyDictionary.org*, April 7, 2013, https://psychologydictionary.org/poverty-of-ideas/

23. Not Falling into Achievement

When achievement is understood as a snare

Zen Master Hongzhi discussed his acting and communicating: "Responding without falling into achievement, speaking without involving listeners."

As a manager you respond, daily, to a wide variety of job demands. You provide guidance, evaluate information, handle disputes, make decisions, give presentations, report upward. Naturally, you put yourself into all these things. You identify with your own actions and words – who doesn't? – and are concerned that they prove effective.

So what is Master Hongzhi talking about? What could it mean to act without "falling into achievement," or – equally perplexing – speak without "involving listeners"? If perplexity is your reaction to Hongzhi's oracular words, let it be said that work psychologists would be right there with you. They have long believed that accomplishing and communicating are important facets of a manager's identity.

Let's take achievement first. One important window onto this has been tagged by psychologists as NAch – Need for Achievement. David McClelland first posited that people differ in some basic needs related to work. Need for Achievement, or NAch, is one. Workers high in NAch show a preference for challenging work over which they can exert some control. This means they are willing to take some risk of failure, because they find work is more engaging, and accomplishment much sweeter, when tasks are harder. A manager low in NAch, on the other hand, prefers a less challenging job, since success is more likely from the word go. Interestingly, McClelland maintained that the drive for accomplishment or NAch could be trained, and carried out research with managers that supported this view. He also posited two other needs or drives that are important to understanding manager behavior. One was Need for Affiliation (NAff), the other NPow – the need for power. NAff, as you might suspect, is the preference for making and maintaining good relations with employees and other members of management. NPow is a drive to take charge and control people and events.

Back to NAch. Christopher Orpen developed a questionnaire to assess achievement needs. His concept of NAch was that it consists of a number of sub-components: desiring to work hard toward goals both personal and professional; seeking the sense of reward that comes from the pursuit and attainment of excellence; enjoying out-competing others who are trying for same goals as oneself; acquiring material and financial rewards; aspiring for status and authority over others; and mastering, for their own sake, difficult challenges.

Which of Orpen's facets of NAch would you say correctly describe you? Because managers do vary in how highly they score on each. In general, however, higher can be expected to be better for some outcomes. Orpen administered his scale to a sample of middle managers and predicted that the facets would correlate with supervisor ratings of the managers' levels of motivation compared to peers, and also the managers' salary growth within the firm. And most did – higher facets of NAch predicted higher rated motivation and salary growth.

So there can be little doubt that some managers will be more driven than others to achieve, and that they will in fact achieve more. The question for us is: when they achieve, do they "fall into achievement"?

Before addressing that, let's ponder Hongzhi's suggestion that we speak "without involving listeners." On the face of it, this advice is diametrically opposed to modern management theory. Yes, originally supervisors and managers assumed communications that were largely one-way (managers/supervisors -> subordinates) were normal and acceptable. Consider Frederick Taylor, famous for his early 20th-century development and application of "scientific management" in factories. He would explain to laborers that all they needed to do to be more efficient (and hence more pleasing to the plant owners) was to obey his guidance. To be fair, workers also made more money under Taylor's system. In any case, he carefully studied a job and determined how the workers' movements could be reduced or made most economical, and the last thing he wanted was a laborer thinking for themselves. Obedience was the thing. "Now stand," he would order. "Now pick up that batch of iron. Now load it onto the train car." And, because his goals could only be met if the laborer was not exhausted, he would also say "Now sit and rest" – the rest time being carefully specified.

But Taylor was old-school. For many years now psychologists have advised managers to ensure that communications with employees are two-way. That is, engage your employees through your communications. Involve them. Make sure they understand what you are saying, uncover their questions. In this way there is a better chance to anticipate problems and recognize any unexpected issues as they arise. For example, in any organizational change effort, it's wise to make sure any obstacles to the proposed change are uncovered as early as possible. This is achieved through careful dialog.

It's not that communications need necessarily to be super frequent. It is the quality, including the two-wayness, that is important. As team researchers Scott Tannenbaum and Eduardo Salas point out, when it comes to communication, "more is not better – better is better." Such communication helps create and maintain an environment of high trust and involvement.

Deeper, more mutual discussions and messaging between management and employees and among employees seems like common sense to us now. We've moved from more hierarchical, less engaged organizations to flatter, more team-oriented ones, where employee involvement is consciously valued.

So, evidence for the normal and often healthy need for achievement among managers on the one hand, and the importance of involving employees in communications, on the other. Should we conclude that Hongzhi had no idea what he was talking about? Probably not.

What can be termed "non-action within action" appears in the writings of many figures such as Master Hongzhi. It is to act or speak from a place of utter stillness, and without attempting to gain anything. Jesus of Nazareth made a similar point: "Do not let the left hand know what the right hand is doing." That is, avoid the inner taking of credit. When you do not take credit, you can act without "falling into achievement" – without seeing yourself as the center of things. Similarly, when you speak without seeking credit, you are not expecting any personal affirmation from your hearers. You have communicated "without involving listeners."

Such an attitude need not mean that you don't wish your actions to have an effect. But you are not attached, as it were, to those hoped-for effects. Nor does such an attitude mean that you don't wish your communications to be without influence. Rather, you are not emotionally committed to their effects.

Importantly, not seeking credit for yourself does not mean you do not credit the accomplishments of others. On the contrary, rewarding and recognizing employees is a central managerial function.

But for oneself, this acting-without-acting and speaking-without-speaking leaves you free. You can do all the things managers need to do but without making it about you. And, if it's not about you, then you will be able to see things without the intervening you-colored glasses. You can see the effects of your actions and words in your organization more clearly and with less anxiety. And others will be better able to appreciate what it is you do and say, since they don't have to disentangle, as it were, those actions and communications from your person. They can focus less on pleasing and reinforcing their manager and attend more to the work at hand. In a way, by "not falling into accomplishment" yourself, you create autonomy for them.

My own opinion is that this is not about "transcending the ego." I suspect such a thing is impossible. Moreover, we've noted that managers activate and benefit from NAch; from characteristics like competitiveness and even acquisitiveness; from the desire to get ahead in the less-than-orderly world that characterizes all organizations. But maybe Master Hongzhi is positing that is possible, not to transcend the ego, but to be less ego-ful, less grabbing, more watchful.

> Master Hongzhi was a famous practitioner and teacher of Chinese Zen, whose life (1091–1157) bridged the Song and Yuan dynasties. He is considered one of the early proponents of the Zen of "Silent Illumination."

Leighton, T. D., & Wu, Y. (2000). *Cultivating the empty field: The silent illumination of Zen master Hongzhi*. Tuttle Publishing.

McClelland, D. C. (2013). That urge to achieve. *Readings and Exercises in Organizational Behavior*, 70-76.

Orpen, C. (1995). The Multifactorial Achievement Scale as a predictor of salary growth and motivation among middle-managers. *Social Behavior and Personality: an international journal, 23(2)*, 159-162.

Tannenbaum, S., & Salas, E. (2020). *Teams that work: the seven drivers of team effectiveness*. Oxford University Press.

24. Manager Without a Title

Philosopher Blaise Pascal – and Zen Master Rinzai – hint at the danger of a title

> "I would prefer you to see no quality till you meet it and have occasion to use it," wrote Blaise Pascal, "for fear some one quality prevail and designate the man."

Everyone has a title, it seems. There is something about them. Some curious uses include "promoting" an employee by titling them a "manager" (exempt) so that overtime cannot be charged. Or, giving AI chatbots human titles such as manager, which seems to increase customer satisfaction with these bots.

Certainly, titles for managers are ubiquitous in the business world and form an endless list: Account Manager, Program Manager, Risk Manager, Technical Services Manager, IT Director, Sales Supervisor, Marketing Manager, General Manager, (add your title here). Such titles serve obvious purposes: they indicate your specialty, degree of authority and status, and perhaps span of control, within an organization. They are a shorthand that everyone understands; without them, each time you attended a meeting, you would have to list your job duties during introductions instead of simply stating your job title. And research finds what we already know – that people use job titles when introducing themselves in informal, non-work settings. In response to "What do you do?", it is simple and useful to say (for example), "Oh, I'm Manager of Events."

Some companies are using more "with it" job titles for managers: Talent and Vibe Manager, Wish Manager, Director of First Impressions, Chief of Chatting. These may be secondary, or "fun" job titles that employees can choose for their own. Researcher Adam Grant and colleagues posit that managers and others felt that "fun" designations have favorable effects. These included perceptions of reduced hierarchical distance, self-affirmation, and a kind of disarming function leading to increased comfort among employees. But "fun" job designators are one thing; problems can occur with formal but non-traditional titles, particularly lack of comparability across companies – which could impact wage surveys, for example.

Job titles, despite their general use, are not always beneficial to the title holder. I once met a person who said to me, "I used to have a Ph.D." This phrase seems to contain a recognition that experience teaches us what we *don't* know. I'm not positive if this was the same individual who told me they had removed their title "Ph.D." from their office door, after finding it only served to complicate rather than help relationships with employees.

This latter point, that a title may be a social hindrance, is intriguing. A title can indicate expertise, but for some employees it also can hold negative ("elite") connotations. And some managers, consciously or unconsciously, buy into the idea of being more important than others. But even if you are modest about your managerial designation, is there still something odd about the whole job title thing?

An essential critique of titles comes from the mystical quarter. It suggests that an identity even slightly defined by a title is fundamentally and utterly mistaken. One reputedly rather fierce Zen Master (Rinzai) said that a person without title (or, of no rank) exists in you, going and coming. "Those who have not witnessed this fact, discover it this minute!" Then there is the Chinese Zen master Linji, who said, "There is a true man with no rank, always present not even a hair's breadth away."

Who is the person of no rank, the individual of no title? It is you, the you *before* and *in spite of* any job identity. Somewhere in you there is a manager of no title, a non-manager manager.

One of the roles of a mystic is to puncture our superficial identities, no matter how important we may seem to be. Here is yet another Zen master carrying out that role:

> Keichu, the great Zen teacher of the Meiji era, was the head of Tofuku, a cathedral in Kyoto. One day the governor of Kyoto called upon him for the first time. His attendant presented the card of the governor, which read: Kitagaki, Governor of Kyoto. "I have no business with such a fellow," said Keichu to his attendant. "Tell him to get out of here." The attendant carried the card back with apologies. "That was my error," said the governor, and with a pencil he scratched out the words Governor of Kyoto. "Ask your teacher again." "Oh, is that Kitagaki?" exclaimed the teacher when he saw the card. "I want to see that fellow."

Of course, governors have to govern and managers manage; we need authority to do that, and our job title indicates some level of power. But can we mentally cross out that title with a pencil, and trust ourselves? People do create, after all, a rather ridiculous spectacle when presenting themselves as "somebody who is somebody." Employees have a nose for such attitudes in managers, and a probable erosion of morale is the result. In the end managerial arrogance can only hamper, not help, productivity.

Blaise Pascal was a French philosopher, mathematician, physicist, and Catholic mystic. He wrote the quote at the top of this chapter in his book called *Pensées*, or thoughts. It was published eight years after his death in 1662. The quote suggests something rather complex, but it is clearly applicable to managers, and it highlights yet another downside to titles.

First, Pascal says "I would prefer you to see no quality till you meet it and have occasion to use it." He isn't speaking of managers specifically, but we can think how this might apply. If we "see no quality" in our employees, I think it means we are not narrowing our understanding of them, and of what they can do, prematurely. We resist making any conclusion based on looks and quirks. It is a kind of negative skill – refraining from judgement (which, incidentally, recalls the words of one greater than Pascal: Do not judge lest you be judged).

In any case, we retain an open mind about an employee, until we "meet" a quality in them and "have occasion to use it." That is, we perceive a level of knowledge, skill, or ability in an employee which can address a current organizational need. And then the role of manager kicks in: you ensure that the employee gets the guidance and support they need in leveraging that knowledge, skill, or ability to succeed in their job. This fits with the relatively recent advice that managers should focus on employee strengths, not weaknesses.

It is important to avoid perceiving and using qualities too quickly, "for fear some one quality prevail and designate the man." That is, before pigeon-holing the employee: she can do X and only X. Such pigeon-holing, such designating, such titling, of the person reduces future possibilities – for them and for you. It may mean you miss the employee's most fundamental strengths.

In sum, the lesson on titles from the mystics seems to be twofold. First, we can't in any way mistake our titles for ourselves. Otherwise, we cannot answer the challenge, "Who are you, aside from your social status and identity?" Second, we must endeavor to avoid categorizing employees too quickly or narrowly. Otherwise, we cannot perceive who they are or might become, aside from the categories we ourselves have created.

Blaise Pascal (1623-1662) accomplished much in his short life. A child prodigy, he contributed to advances in geometry and probability. He invented a mechanical calculator. After becoming a Jansenist (Jansenism was a Catholic movement), he wrote philosophic and religious works. At the age of 31 he had a profoundly moving mystical experience and ever after privately carried with him a note about the experience; the beginning of the note – found after his death – explains: "From about half past ten at night until about half past midnight, FIRE."

Cohen, L., Gurun, U., & Ozel, N. B. (2023). *Too many managers: The strategic use of titles to avoid overtime payments* (No. w30826). National Bureau of Economic Research.

Grant, A. M., Berg, J. M., & Cable, D. M. (2014). Job titles as identity badges: How self-reflective titles can reduce emotional exhaustion. *Academy of Management Journal, 57(4)*, 1201-1225.

Jeon, Y. A. (2022). Let me transfer you to our AI-based manager: Impact of manager-level job titles assigned to AI-based agents on marketing outcomes. *Journal of Business Research, 145*, 892-904.

Pascal, Blaise (1958) *Pascal's Pensees - A justification of Christianity that is a masterpiece of religious philosophy*. New York: E.P. Dutton.

Washi, Taka. *122 Zen Koans: Find enlightenment*. (2013). Edited and translated by Taka Washi, Kindle book, Case 30, location 342.

25. The Dose Counts: Are You Being Too Supportive?

Oddly enough, managers can learn from medieval physician and alchemist Paracelsus

Medieval itinerant physician and mystic Paracelsus used to say, "Only the dose permits something not to be poisonous."

Would it surprise you to hear that managers can act in "destructive" ways? That they might sometimes undermine a company's and/or employees' best interests? I presume that you would say something like, "No, I'm not surprised. Of course, managers can have negative effects. Some are abusive, others lazy or incompetent, for example."

But what if you were told that destructive leadership is fairly common? To me, that is a surprising (and somewhat disturbing) finding.

Management researchers Ståle Einarsen, Merethe Aasland, Anders Skogstad and colleagues report on this topic. Before addressing the prevalence of destructive management, however, let's look at their model. It is based on two dimensions, one running from anti-organization behavior to pro-organization behavior, the other from anti-subordinate behavior to pro-subordinate behavior. This creates four defining quadrants, plus one center identifier. Of these five, four represent poor management styles (below I've replaced "Leadership" with "Management"):

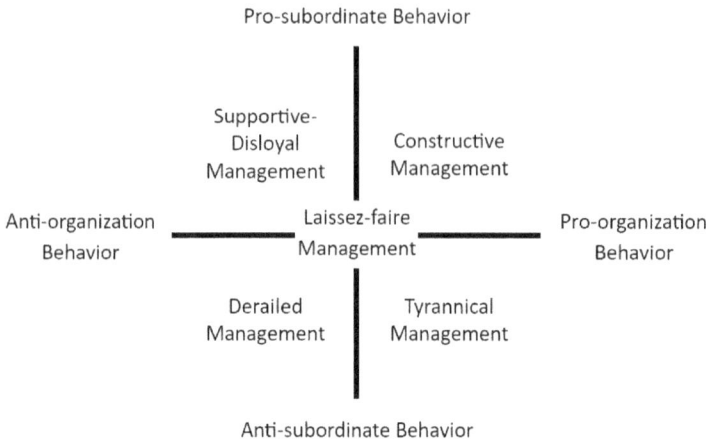

Pro-subordinate Behavior

	Supportive- Disloyal Management	Constructive Management	
Anti-organization Behavior	Laissez-faire Management		Pro-organization Behavior
	Derailed Management	Tyrannical Management	

Anti-subordinate Behavior

The upper right quadrant: "Constructive Management" represents the place where good managers live. Their behaviors support both employees and the organization.

The lower right quadrant, "Tyrannical Management," defines those managers who behave badly toward employees but are supportive of the legitimate goals of the organization. One might think that it is not possible to be supportive of the organization while treating employees poorly. However, consider the task-driven manager who routinely expects subordinates to work uncompensated overtime, micromanages, or even belittles them in his effort to generate maximum productivity. From an employee's point of view, this manager might indeed be tyrannical, while company leadership may be delighted with his or her department exceeding goals in KPI's.

"Derailed" managers (lower left quadrant) are those who succeed in both damaging worker morale and well-being through negative employee-directed behaviors and also damage the organization through theft, corruption, absenteeism, fraud, and so forth. These managers are "derailed" because they are completely off the track – their behaviors are virtually completely negative.

"Laissez-faire" managers (center) demonstrate little positive or negative behaviors. They let things ride.

Finally, there is the quadrant labeled "Supportive-Disloyal." This is the one that is most intriguing to me, since it highlights a relatively undiscussed style of management. Here, a manager is oriented toward employee well-being. But the support and encouragement given to subordinates is not such that it helps the overall organization. Perhaps employees are provided unearned or excessive rewards. Perhaps their needs (e.g., time off, longer times available to complete tasks) are granted without any consideration of whether the legitimate needs of the company are met. Truly inefficient work habits may be overlooked or even encouraged. At the extreme, employees may be encouraged to defraud the company in some way.

"Supportive." We don't usually think of that as describing management behavior in a negative way. But maybe Paracelsus has something to teach us in this regard.

Paracelsus was a remarkable figure. Astrologist and itinerant physician, he inveighed against many of the standard medical conventions and authorities. He is famous for burning, in the town square, books of Galen and Avicenna. Both of these figures were famous philosophers and physicians (one Muslim, the other Greek) and their works were considered in the time of Paracelsus to be authoritative and correct.

One of his sayings is quoted at the top of this chapter, "Only the dose permits something not to be poisonous." Note that he is not only saying something bad, given in small doses, may not be poisonous. (This actually is the philosophy of Mithridatism, where one develops tolerance to toxins over time by receiving small doses). Instead, the thought I want to highlight is that Paracelsus is suggesting that that *everything* can be poisonous; it simply depends on the amount.

Is this true of managerial niceness? That is, is it possible to be too nice? The quadrant model above suggests that this is what happens in the "Supportive – Disloyal" quadrant: supportive to employees to the extent of disloyalty to the company and its mission.

In terms of how many managers fall into each category, Aasland and colleagues found that between one third and almost two-thirds of employees reported frequent and consistent negative behaviors in their immediate supervisors. Specifically, about 9% of employees report working under "derailed" leaders; about 21% under "laissez-faire" management, and 3.5% under tyrannical managers.

The prevalence of "Supportive-disloyal" leadership, our focus in this chapter, was 11.5%. This is not insignificant, but this negative style of managing is little discussed. It raises the question whether, in an age of tolerance, tolerance can be taken too far.

One wonders what employees really want in managers – niceness or competence. Ideally, of course, both would be present, in which case managers dwell in the upper right quadrant: they are, simply, *constructive*. They aid the organization, and they aid employees.

What is wrong, precisely, with an excess of niceness? Well, employee development could be hampered since employees may be allowed to coast, seeing nary a real challenge. The feedback they get is false: nice, but too nice for poor behavior to be pointed out. Such feedback is inactionable for employees, they have no insight into shortcomings or how to rectify these.

Gareth Gardiner wrote a book entitled *Tough-Minded Management: A Guide for Managers Who are Too Nice for Their Own Good*. He makes many good points, but among them is that managers are sometimes too nice simply because they want to avoid any conflict or discomfort. But he argues too that challenging situations can be handled in a respectful, non-apologetic way. That way one avoids overdosing employees with kindness, while promoting a supportive, just workplace.

Paracelsus (1493-1541) was an iconoclast. He was a physician, "father of toxicology," and prophet. For him, discoveries in science were communications from God, and humans have a duty to uncover them.

Aasland, M. S., Skogstad, A., Notelaers, G., Nielsen, M. B., & Einarsen, S. (2010). The prevalence of destructive leadership behaviour. *British Journal of Management*, *21*(2), 438-452.

Einarsen, S., Aasland, M. S., & Skogstad, A. (2007). Destructive leadership behaviour: A definition and conceptual model. *The Leadership Quarterly, 18(3)*, 207-216.

Gardiner, G. S. (1993). *Tough-minded management: A guide for managers who are too nice for their own good*. Fawcett.

26. Management and the Emotions of Envy and Schadenfreude

A blind farmer helps us see the possibility of dealing with some common human failings

> A blind man lived near Master Bankei's temple. Because he could not see people's faces or posture, he had to judge their character by the sound of their voices alone. After Bankei died, the man made an interesting observation. He said that, among those he heard commenting on another's good fortune, only in Bankei's voice did he hear no envy. And only in the Master's voice did he hear no satisfaction when referring to another's plight.

Envy is usually thought of in wholly negative terms, as in this definition: a "painful or resentful awareness of an advantage or possession enjoyed by another and the desire to possess the same thing." It can, though, have a positive meaning, as in a simple *motivating* recognition of another's advantage or possession. So, for example, if another manager has a certification in Total Quality Management and you see that as a benefit to her, you may jump online to obtain the same certification. In this case, envy is just the recognition of a kind of discrepancy that you would like to rectify. Clearly this second flavor of envy is not destructive; the first can be. We'll focus, though, in this brief chapter on the first version of envy, the one with the negative character.

Whereas envy can prompt feelings of irritation and insecurity, there is another emotion which is pleasant, but just as bad for us as envy. This is "schadenfreude," a "pleasure derived from another person's misfortune." Whereas envy is a painful comparison to the fortunes and circumstances of others (I am looking up at a fortunate other, as it were, and hence feeling insecure and lacking), schadenfreude is a pleasant comparison (since I am looking down from a secure position toward another's lack or misfortune). In a sense, then, these emotions are siblings – it just depends on whether one is looking up or down, up to another's good fortune, or down to another's misfortune.

Even though schadenfreude may be pleasurable, it is not an honorable pleasure.

I would also say these emotions are both common and completely natural. Raise your hand (or text me) if you have experienced neither! I'll get some kind of certificate together.

Still – and here the mystics stake out some territory difficult to reach – the natural and even normal darker sides to who we are need not define us. We can get better, in the sense of experiencing envy and schadenfreude less or possibly even – if the story of Bankei is to be trusted – eliminating them.

Read the short narrative about Bankei at the top of this chapter again. Bankei feels wholly good at the good fortune of another and feels no satisfaction at the misfortune of another. If I put aside any cynicism about whether such a state is achievable, I am struck by how desirable it would be to possess a character such as this.

It's a curious thing that the workplace is precisely the kind of environment that would be expected to produce envy and schadenfreude in ourselves and in our employees. This is because there are – no matter how "flat" your organization – differences in rank and hierarchy. Unless you are on the absolute top, there is always someone above you to look up at. In a similar way, unless you are on the absolute bottom, you can always find others below you to look down on. In addition, it is common for workers to be rewarded and sanctioned differentially, based on perceived performance, preference, bias, and the like. Whether above or below, there are "winners" and "losers."

So, given hierarchy and differential rewards and inevitable differential circumstances, we can say with certainty that envy and its sibling, schadenfreude, are common in the workplace.

Yet they are rarely discussed. Certainly, management training hardly ever addresses these topics. Is this because they are harmless? I would say not, since they can motivate unkind and even injurious words and actions. Are envy and schadenfreude considered "out of bounds" since they are part of the private interior life of managers and employees and even unlikely to be changed? This may be the case.

Work researcher Yolanda Na Li and colleagues examined a particular situation where a manager can be afflicted by envy: that in which there are employees who perform very well. So well, in fact, that they cross some interior or mental line in the manager's mind. This triggers envy on the manager's part, and this in turn can unleash negative and even abusive management behaviors.

These researchers suggest some ways to handle this. They propose, for example, that perhaps managers can be somehow made less aware of excellent performance on the part of employees. This might be done by letting AI carry out the performance management (rating the employees' performance, say) part of the manager's job. This might or not be feasible. They suggest too that organizations identify and intervene when manager emotions become negative. Again, this might be difficult to accomplish or intrusive if accomplished. But Li and colleagues also indicate that a couple of approaches more likely to succeed at reducing management envy. The first is training to help managers identify and manage their own envy. The second is to place above the highest performing employees managers who are low in the tendency to make social comparisons. There are scales that purport to measure this tendency.

However, given the ubiquity of envy and schadenfreude, the best course may simply be to try to minimize these in our inner self. How to do that?

Presumably, it reduces to the fundamental question of overcoming self-centeredness. This usually occurs via cultivating meditation, humility, prayer, and reflection.

Bankei Yōtaku (1622-1693) was a Zen monk and abbot.

Gibbons, F. X., & Buunk, B. P. (1999). Individual differences in social comparison: Development of a scale of social comparison orientation. *Journal of Personality and Social Psychology*, 76(1), 129–142.

Li, Y. N., Law, K. S., Zhang, M. J., & Yan, M. (2023). The mediating roles of supervisor anger and envy in linking subordinate performance to abusive supervision: A curvilinear examination. *Journal of Applied Psychology*. Advance online publication. https://doi.org/10.1037/apl0001141

Reps, P., & Senzaki, N. (1998*). Zen flesh, Zen bones: A collection of Zen and pre-Zen writings*. Tuttle Publishing.

27. Management Science or Management Scientism?

Alfred North Whitehead points out that science should never try to reduce reality to a "mere" reality

> For us the red glow of the sunset should be as much part of nature as are the molecules and electric waves by which men of science would explain the phenomenon. – A. N. Whitehead

One of the interesting things about this quote by philosopher Alfred North Whitehead is that he is returning the individual, non-scientist, human to a central role in reality. The sunset, he is saying, does not *belong* to science or scientists any more than it does to the single, untrained, observer. Science can certainly explain a sunset in many ways – diffractions and reflections of light of varying wavelengths and angles among clouds of varying types with specific humidities, etc. – but these explanations do not *replace* the aesthetic experience of an ordinary, non-analytic observer.

True, the perceptions of our observer are necessarily limited. She is seeing and responding to only a specific sunset, not describing the general phenomena of sunsets. She is paying appreciative attention, and perhaps experiencing very "non-scientific" reactions: awe, say, or pleasure. But it is also true that any analytic, objective description of the sunset must itself be limited, leaving out any number of variables. But both the individual and the scientific perspective can claim validity.

The problem lies in this, that some scientists are ready to say that scientific explanation is somehow more true than normal, everyday experience. But pushing science ahead like that is not *science*, but *scientism*.

Scientism is characterized by the view that the scientific method is the only way to gain understanding. Relatedly, it seems to posit that understanding gained by this method will result in something original. So a scientistic approach to gaining knowledge about how to manage others better than they are currently might say: this can only be done by obtaining new information via the scientific method. Hence the myriad of researchers attempting to apply the scientific method to develop new models and explanations for how managers can best guide and interact with employees.

But this can exclude or undercut other ways of understanding management.

Nothing is wrong with Management Science, except that it sometimes morphs into Management *Scientism*. In both approaches, the belief is that the organization can be analyzed, and principles and models of management derived. But in the scientistic (rather than scientific) view, these principles and models are *the* truth. They possess, it is claimed, the character of objectivity. Not only this, but these principles and models tend to become more elaborate and abstract over time. And these sophisticated models, among scientistic-ists (rather than scientists), are given more credence perhaps than reality itself.

If this seems odd, it is. As philosopher Iaian McGilchrist pointed out,

> The cerebral and the abstract – for example, management and its systems – have become more highly valued than the hands-on task that management exists to serve, with the odd effect that the higher you rise in your craft, skill or profession, the more you will be removed from its performance in order to manage it.

In a sense, scientism is our bent toward developing and wielding tools – we are a toolmaking, tool-leveraging species – taken to an extreme. So, for example, scientistic management researchers have some hypotheses on how to model the workplace (its morale or climate, its efficiency or effectiveness). Then they obtain from their work some tools, techniques, interventions, programs, practices, procedures, or instruments to study whether these might improve things. They carry out research and publish and perhaps do show some applied success. Convinced, HR deploys the approved approaches, usually only to find eventually that something seems to be wrong about the whole thing. And what is left is a kind of dysfunction within the organization that perhaps didn't need to be there at all.

A good example of this is found in the history of Performance Management – by which I mean those activities carried out to assess, and try to maintain and improve, employee job performance. Previous chapters went into this in some detail.

The history of mysticism is, in part, the highlighting of the limits of formalized systems (such as Performance Management). It is not that there is not some rationale for the systems, but that they often become an end in themselves. One major theme we see in the teachings of Jesus of Nazareth was that people are more important to God than rules or systems. It is not that rules are to be ignored – they are meant to guide and support us – but that they should not be degraded into weapons with which to hurt others.

You will learn a lot when you attend management seminars, e-courses, conventions or use tools and techniques designed for managing. But you are learning or using systems and models, and the application of these to the workplace can confuse or create negative effects as well as aid. It seems important to try to return always to the big picture, to what is right in front of you.

Recall the sunset of A.N. Whitehead – it is perceived and "understood" by the untrained. It can be "understood" in a scientific way too, but as soon as that scientific perception is said to be more true than that of the naive observer, we enter the realm of falsehood.

The seeming authority of science can be intimidating or simply very attractive. As Ludwig Wittgenstein –echoing Whitehead – said, we are "irresistibly tempted to ask and answer questions in the way science does ... [but] it can never be our job to reduce anything to anything."

Wittgenstein here is speaking of philosophy, but it may apply to us too. Avoiding the scientistic temptation to reduce the complexity of the workplace would mean that we need to interact with employees and other managers frequently. You won't get along with them, manage them, by techniques or tools or theories, but by observing, listening, and simply managing. This brings us back to the concept of developing expertise the only possible way – by practice. As Wittgenstein also said, "What one acquires here [in application] is not a technique; one learns correct judgments. There are also rules, but they do not form a system, and only experienced people can apply them right."

There are rules, but they should not rule us; we should discover their inmost meaning.

> Alfred North Whitehead (1861-1947) was a mathematician and a philosopher. He challenged the scientific materialism so prevalent during his life, and suggested that the universe, rather than being made up of unchanging objects, is best understood in terms of change. Everything changes; all is process. Hence his philosophy was termed process philosophy.

Whitehead, Alfred North. 1920. *The concept of nature*. Cambridge: Cambridge University Press.

Wittgenstein, L. (1958). *Philosophical investigations*. Oxford: Blackwell.

Wittgenstein, L. (1958). *The blue and brown books*. Oxford: Blackwell.

28. A Clean Break: When Managers Retire

A Zen teacher shows how to leave the stage

> Tanzan wrote sixty postcards on the last day of his life, and asked an attendant to mail them. Then he passed away. The cards read:
>
> *I am departing from this world. This is my last announcement.*
>
> *Tanzan*
>
> *27 July 1892*

There are times in a manager's career that require a clean break from the current state. This might include transfer, promotion, quitting, retirement. Or death, as in Tanzan's case.

We deal with death and management specifically in the Chapter 30. In this one, I'd like to extract and highlight one of the undertones in Tanzan's last statement. That is, simply, the art of making the cleanest possible transition to a new state.

When we leave a job for a new one, it is something of a "shock to the system," as they say. We have a set of routines, duties, friends, and environments; these have in a sense become part of us. It is as if we have been woven or knitted into a large fabric made up of our expectations, memories, emotions, and habits – along with the expectations, memories, emotions, and habits of employees, leaders, and other managers. Leaving is a pulling away of all these interconnecting threads. We can be disoriented for a time.

A new job, though, is one thing – here, at least, we can recreate our identity along similar lines as in our previous occupation. Moreover, in some cases we may have the opportunity to maintain bridges with our erstwhile colleagues. Most people will be able to manage this transition, though it may take time to fully readapt and adjust.

Retirement, however, is another beast altogether. Here there is also a severing from the workplace with all its duties and relationships, both pleasant and unpleasant. But the severing is more severe.

One of the factors that may determine the degree of severity of the movement into retirement is whether it is voluntary or involuntary. If freely chosen, retirement will still be a big deal, but it may not have some of the dark clouds that hover over one that is not so chosen. In the latter case (involuntary retirement), managers find themselves in the same position as their own subordinates, when these are let go.

Interestingly, many economists hold to an idea of an equivalence between employees on the one hand, and organizations, on the other. Theoretically, they maintain, companies can hire and fire, and employees can sign on and leave. But as Elizabeth Anderson points out, there really is no symmetry here: workers are at a disadvantage for any number of reasons, including immediate need for income and penalties associated with voluntary leaving – such as those encoded in Do Not Compete or Do Not Disparage "agreements." Managers too can sense this asymmetry when they ponder leaving their company. As Anderson vividly puts it, to assume symmetry between employer and worker just because the latter is free to leave employ, is false. To claim such symmetry would be to suggest that "wherever individuals are free to exit a relationship, authority cannot exist within it. This is like saying that Mussolini was not a dictator, because Italians could emigrate."

Generally, workers, including managers, think about retiring when they are somewhat older. What are the characteristics of older workers as perceived by managers themselves? Researcher Kene Henkens found, in a large sample of managers, that they perceived older workers along three dimensions: productivity, reliability, and adaptability. Older employees were viewed as less productive only in a few ways compared to younger employees: they were less capable of physical work, less able "to keep up," and less enterprising. They were less interested in participating in training programs, as one might expect (though not necessarily accept as a good thing). In terms of adaptability, they fell behind younger workers: less interested in technological change and less able to adapt to those changes. Older employees were seen as somewhat more reliable than younger employees: they were perceived as more careful.

These perceptions of older workers hint at some of the reasons that people retire when they get to a certain age. Gradually it may be borne in upon a person that they are surrounded by younger workers – perhaps subordinates – who are more energetic and enterprising, more intrigued with new technologies and more able to adapt to those technologies, and more willing to put in time developing themselves. "Is it time to retire?" is a reasonable question in this case.

Of course, this is exactly the question that may be unwelcome, and thus repressed or denied. "Maybe I've lost a step, but I'm still very productive!" What if, however, one stopped after "Maybe I've lost a step" and let that really sink in. I write this because there is something of a phenomenon of people staying in their jobs because of inertia rather than for any really good reason. Suppose a younger person could take your job and actually do it more energetically, with more enterprise, and deploying the full phalanx of new technology. Wouldn't it make sense to step aside?

I think what I'm suggesting in all of this is that the attitude of Tanzan departing this life is a good attitude for departing the life of work. A clean break.

It isn't that managers won't need to adapt to the new reality that is retirement. They will, and that takes time. But to have the courage to enter that new life boldly and cleanly is the thing.

There is a famous story about the Greek general Alexander the Great. In Gordium in Phrygia there was a massive, complicated rope knot which no one had been able to untie. The people held the belief, though, that he who could untie it would be the one who would conquer Asia. Alexander came and examined the knot. Unexpectedly drawing his sword, he sliced it cleanly in two.

Something like this pertains to retirement. And perhaps death, too.

> Hara Tanzan (1819-1892) was a Japanese philosophy teacher and Sōtō (quiet school) Buddhist monk. He attempted to address what he saw as deficiencies in Buddhist descriptions of the physical processes of consciousness by drawing upon Western medical science.

Henkens, K. (2005). Stereotyping older workers and retirement: The managers' point of view. *Canadian Journal on Aging/La Revue canadienne du vieillissement*, 24(4), 353-366.

Anderson, E. (2017). *Private government: How employers rule our lives (and why we don't talk about it)*. Princeton University Press.

Senzaki, N., and Reps, P. (1940). *101 Zen Stories*. Philadelphia, David McKay Company, 1940.

29. Workplace as Sick Ward

Maybe we shouldn't be too smug about our "health"

> "It is not the healthy who need a doctor, but the sick." – Jesus of Nazareth
>
> "I can see no great reason for self-satisfaction because one's strength is rather above the average of those in the same hospital." – Seneca

Many will say that we should fill our minds with self-affirming statements. That we have a right to feel good about ourselves and that being negative or down on ourselves is obviously a bad way to achieve that good feeling. Moreover, some people often do feel fine, and for them it can go against the grain – and common sense – to believe that they are ill when they are clearly not.

And, as Jesus says, if you believe you are healthy and happy you will not feel you need a physician. Who goes to the doctor when well (aside from those annual "checkups")? No one.

But we can be well in some surface sense while ill in a deeper sense. I think this is what the Roman senator and Stoic Philosopher Seneca is pointing out. He envisions the world as a hospital, with everyone needing a cure. But in this hospital of the world, only some of the patients are aware that they are sick. Others maintain that they are fully and robustly healthy. "So what?" we can imagine Seneca saying to these "healthy" people. "Your boast of good health is nothing more than stating you are in above average condition among all patients – you are simply saying, after all, that you are less sick than many. Why is that a source of satisfaction to you, given after all that you have contracted the same illness as everyone else?"

What's curious about this line of thought is that it seems to put at advantage those who admit that they are ill. For these people, who recognize their sickness, will not refuse assistance. To these, the nature, number, and skill of the attending physicians will be of utmost importance. These patients will listen carefully to their doctors and follow their advice and prescriptions. They may be on their way to getting better.

On the other hand, those who count themselves healthy, to never have been sick in the first place, are unlikely to even recognize that they are in a hospital. They certainly will not seek out or follow advice on how to get better, since they don't believe they need any betterment.

The "healthy," Seneca seems to say, are not just sick like everyone else, they are also deluded.

Based on both Jesus' and Seneca's words, we might thus divide any group of people into two. There are those who have at least to some extent acknowledged that they are damaged, sick, incomplete, and in need. Then there are those who deny this, and who may even believe that it is sickness to suggest that one is sick. For the first, help is offered. For the second, they will proceed without such aid.

Perhaps we think that those in the second group are to be envied for their (self-asserted) well-being. Aren't they the happy ones, who do not go about with any sense of being damaged? They are the happy ones -- *unless* Seneca the Roman has put his finger on the real pulse of that group. In that case, they ought – for their own good! – seek out and identify their sickness, for it is there.

But how is that to be done? How to get to grips with the real nature of things? Looking around at things is a start. That's what Buddha did.

The story of Gotama Buddha includes a preface, in which he is a prince, living in luxury and protected from bad news of all kinds. Upon leaving his palace, though, he is confronted with an old person, a sick person, and a dead person. For him, the world is suddenly transformed into something very different from a palace. Now it has become a hospital, and not only a hospital, but a hospice and a morgue. The harshness of this reality – previously hidden from him – creates in him a desire to discover a way out. One of the "ways out" in Buddhism is to meditate on exactly old age, sickness, and death so that the impermanence of the world and of our lives is deeply ingrained in our awareness.

So the first suggestion is that we first look out at the world. Then too, look inward. Doing so cannot help but bring not only one's strengths to mind but one's deficiencies and weaknesses. But, the mystics seem to say, it is not just *imperfection* but *illness* that can be seen when contemplating our inner self. Ludwig Wittgenstein even made this perception a gauge of one's spirituality. "People," he wrote, "are religious to the extent that they believe themselves to be not so much *imperfect*, as *ill*."

How might this discussion of a psychic illness, of the world as hospital, scale to the workplace as sick ward? There are, I think, several ways.

First, the recognition and pondering of general suffering has an effect. It acts to highlight what might be called "universal vulnerability." No one, no matter how seemingly psychologically hale and indestructible, is fully so in reality. Once this is recognized, we can see that, as Seneca says, there is little room for justified boasting. In fact, it may be the smug who are most in line for a downfall, whether soon or late.

Similarly, a deep acknowledgment of universal vulnerability can help foster a perceptive compassion toward others. It may make it easier to see the suffering which many seek to hide. This in turn means that politeness and tact are key managerial attributes.

A perception of universal vulnerability also means that we can sense that we are all in the same boat, all managers, all employees. True, the boat is actually a hospital ship. But the sense of the oneness of our condition and fate should aid, not hinder our communications and teamwork. A sense of self-importance will act to separate us from others; a sense of shared existential pain can unite.

Compassion is not equal to depression. While recognizing pervasive suffering *out there*, and a profound impairment *in here* can lead to some somber periods in a person's life, these should not be ultimately paralyzing or debilitating. That is because there is help within this hospital, and being helped, we can help.

Jesus (0 BCE to 33 CE) is regarded by Christians everywhere as savior of the world.

Seneca (c. 4 BCE – 65 CE) was a Roman philosopher, teacher, and political figure. He was tutor to the young Nero, who later became Ceasar. In the aftermath of a conspiracy – in which Seneca was likely not involved – in 65 CE Nero ordered Seneca to kill himself, which he did.

New International Version. Mark 2:17

Seneca the Younger. (1910). *Physical science in the time of Nero, a translation of the quaestiones naturales Of Seneca* J. Clarke trans. Macmillan and Co., Limited.

Wittgenstein, L. (1980). *Culture and value*. GH von Wright and H. Nyman, eds. P. Winch, trans. Oxford: Blackwell.

30. Death and Management

Should we think about death or not?

> "The disinclination to understand death is no different from the disinclination of a man to subject himself to a medical check-up although he feels that something is wrong with him." - V. F. Gunaratna
>
> "If on the other hand you accept the word of Ecclesiastes that there is 'no better thing under the sun, than to eat, and to drink, and to be merry,' you may wish to leave the question of death to be answered only when necessary." – B. F. Skinner

V. F. Gunaratna and B. F. Skinner have opposing views on whether it makes sense to ponder our death. The Buddhist provides a firm endorsement, suggesting that if we do not, we are avoiding a healthy topic, in the way that a person avoids going to the doctor. Skinner demurs.

Before going further, here is a question you may have: Why talk about death with managers? There are a couple of reasons that such a discussion might be appropriate. First, if for one-third (at least) of our waking hours we are working, critical topics will intrude whether we want them to or not. Second, managers will face death via employees who lose family, co-workers who die, or death may come very close to home in managers' own lives – as when parents or other loved ones die. It's not that one is ever truly prepared for such events, but we can at least be more prepared than we might have been. We recognize death is part of life, as it were.

However that may be, let's reflect on Gunaratna's view first. In the quote above, Gunaratna puts his finger on something. I have observed that death is, in fact, rarely a welcome topic of discussion. People seem disinclined to consider it.

And why wouldn't they be so disinclined? There are obvious reasons for avoiding the topic; these reasons are at least reasonable on the surface. Thinking or talking about death doesn't make it less inevitable, so what is the point? Plus, why focus on that when there is so much living to do? Doesn't a preoccupation with death simply degrade our current experience by causing useless anxiety? Moreover, wouldn't we say that such an obsession is morbid and unhealthy, and may even lead to many undesirable behaviors? For example, a person might be preoccupied with death in such a way to engender a deep fear of it. This, it seems, could result in avoiding everyday activities such as going for a walk – since there is a chance of being hit by a car when crossing a street.

Yet Gunaratna is suggesting that avoiding thoughts of death is like avoiding a medical checkup. If you feel there is something physically wrong with you, it's only reasonable to go to the doctor. If we sense something wrong in our psychology, perhaps we go to a therapist. But what if what is wrong is deeper than the purely physical and psychological? This should spur an examination, not an evasion. And a close examination will entail thinking about death.

The argument that death should be pondered is hardly restricted to Eastern thinking. *Memento mori*, Latin for "remember you must die," has long been a cultural meme in the West. Monks might keep a human skull in their cell as a spur to meditation on the transitory nature of life. Contemplating death was in fact recommended by many Christian saints, including Ignatius of Loyola. Socrates, according to Plato, argued that the goal of philosophy is to prepare for dying and death. The Stoic philosophers thought the same thing. The 16th century humanist Michel de Montaigne wrote, "To begin depriving death of its greatest advantage over us, let us deprive death of its strangeness, let us frequent it, let us get used to it; let us have nothing more often in mind than death."

So what is it, exactly, about a steady awareness of death that might be helpful? Perhaps we can listen a bit more to V. F. Gunaratna. He quotes an ancient Buddhist text (the *Visuddhi Magga*):

> The disciple who devotes himself to this contemplation of death is always vigilant, takes no delight in any form of existence, gives up hankering after life, censures evil doing, is free from craving as regards the requisites of life, his perception of impermanence becomes established, he realizes the painful and soulless nature of existence and at the moment of death he is devoid of fear, and remains mindful and self-possessed. Finally, if in this present life he fails to attain Nibbāna [Nirvana], upon the dissolution of the body he is bound for a happy destiny.

This, of course, is a specific Buddhist take on the value of this activity. But a few general benefits can be extracted: vigilance, mindfulness, and self-possession; deep perspective regarding cravings and graspings; awareness of the impermanence of things; lack of fear.

Ideally, then, it seems that pondering death can bring perspective and balance, with peace and collectedness a result of that perspective. This might be because it brings to the surface psychic discomforts which might haunt us if repressed. Or, it might be because it forces us to examine what we believe (and others believe) about death and life after death.

On the other hand, behavioral psychologist Skinner argues that thinking about death can be counterproductive. Specifically, it can engender fear, and that fear can make life less enjoyable. He says elsewhere, "What arouses fear is not death itself, but the act of talking and thinking about it, and that can be stopped… you can turn your attention away from death." You do this by changing the focus of your attention. Do something interesting: talk to others (not about death), go to a meeting or training class, write reports or analyze data, review the performance of your employees. Because "we brood about death when we have nothing else to do… The more reason we have to pay attention to life, the less we have to pay attention to death."

Just as I feel Gunaratna has put his finger on something, so I think Skinner has put his on something else. Maybe there is a time to every season, a time to recognize, consider, and embrace the topic of death, and a time to think and talk about anything but!

V. F. Gunaratna (1905-1977) received an education in Law in Colombo, Sri Lanka. He served as lawyer and as judge – in which role he reportedly adjudicated settlements to the benefit of all parties.

B. F. Skinner (1904-1990) was one of the founders of the psychological school called *behaviorism*. He believed, based on his and others' experiments, that human behavior – like all behavior – could be explained by its consequences, which caused actions to increase or decrease in frequency and strength.

Gunaratna, V. F. (1966). *Buddhist reflections on death* (Vol. 14). Kandy, Ceylon: Buddhist Publication Society.

Montaigne, M. E. (1958). *The complete essays of Montaigne*. Stanford University Press.

Skinner, B. F., & Vaughan, M. E. (1997). *Enjoy old age: A practical guide*. WW Norton & Company.

31. *Duc in Altum*! – Set out into the Deep!

Despite everything, boldness is worthwhile

> "*Duc in altum*! These words ring out for us today, and they invite us to remember the past with gratitude, to live the present with enthusiasm and to look forward to the future with confidence." – St. John Paul II
>
> "All will be well, and all will be well and all manner of thing will be well."
> - Julian of Norwich

Having just thought about death and management in the previous chapter, in this last we think about life and management. To do that, we start with two quotes from two well-known Christians: St. John Paul II and Julian of Norwich.

John Paul II's "*Duc in altum*" comes from the Latin version of Luke's gospel. Christ here encourages his soon-to-be disciples to literally put out into the deep sea. Following his command, they catch many fish.

While the words of John Paul above were written specifically to Christians and rely on Christ for full validity, his words may nonetheless have a resonance that can be heard by everyone. *Gratitude* for the past, *enthusiasm* for the present, and *confidence* for the future. The 263rd, and first Slavic, pope, John Paul II embodied in his life these characteristics. If we strive to embody them ourselves, can we go far wrong?

John Paul II mentions gratitude, enthusiasm and confidence. Gratitude in the workplace is associated with increased performance, motivation, and contentment, and decreased mistreatment. There are measures or interventions that can increase gratitude. These include journaling activities which encourage the documenting of things for which one is grateful, behavioral expressed gratitude interventions such as writing a letter to a benefactor, and educational efforts that include discussions and role-playing.

Enthusiasm for the present is another way of defining motivation and engagement, which we have touched on several places in this book.

But what about confidence in the future, John Paul's third goal for us? Time to consider the words of Julian of Norwich.

This famous quote from Julian ("All will be well, and all will be well and all manner of thing will be well") was received by her in a vision. Post-vision, she labored to understand the words for a decade and a half. Given this, it is unlikely that I or you will be able to grasp it in its fullness without similar time commitment.

Julian was an "anchoress," living in a dedicated cell attached to a church in Norwich, England. Though she is not officially canonized, this is likely just a matter of time. The brief excerpt above – as I say, by far the most famous – comes from Julian's *Shewings* ("Showings" or "What has been Shown").

The quote is appropriate for us to consider in this short book for three reasons. First, it is a statement of unlimited optimism, and gives us a chance to talk about optimism and management – even if we can't pierce all its implications. Second, it is authoritative in the mystical sense. Julian carefully recorded her visions and her thoughts about them, and her historical existence bridging the 14th and 15th centuries is unquestioned. Third, it is a beautiful statement that already has significant cultural impact, in literature and song.

Naturally, optimism as is usually studied in work psychology is more prosaic and earth-bound. Some believe that it can be trained.

Optimism can be understood as a "state" – a temporary mental attitude – and also as a "trait." To have trait optimism is to have a life-long tendency in that direction. In both cases, optimism is characterized by a belief that good things are likely to happen in the future, and that current and future obstacles can be overcome.

So, one can be in general optimistic (trait) and thus likely to experience state optimism much of the time, or one may not be optimistic in a general sense, but still experience optimism depending on context.

Trait optimism is beneficial in that it seems to lead to better outcomes, both globally as in better mental and physical health, and more specifically in such events as recovery after surgery and quality of postoperative life. Results like these are reported in well-conducted studies that follow people over decades (for example, studies such as those carried out by Toshihiko Maruta and colleagues).

Important for our purposes, optimism also seems to be related to job performance. This makes sense, given that optimists should interpret work difficulties more as challenges than as simply obstacles – they see them as temporary bumps in the road. It is thus likely to relate to perseverance.

Granting that optimism is good for both employees and for work outcomes, an important question is: can we work to improve optimism – increase "state" optimism – among our workers?

Research suggests that this is possible to some extent. Psychologist Martin Seligman argues for "learned optimism." For him, optimists see problems and bad events as temporary, with external causes. They believe that good events are due to more personal or lasting causes. They recover more quickly from setbacks and can even overstate the control they have over events. Cognitive therapy, he believed, can build optimism. The provision of sufficient resources, emotional support, and help in framing challenging circumstances are all managerial actions that can encourage and sustain optimism.

Still, where does the optimism come from, that lets us take the risk of putting out into the deep? We need to be encouraged to do this, for the deep is the dark, the unknown. But unless we set out into it, we will remain just where we are, and who we are.

Duc in altum!

St. John Paul II (Karol Józef Wojtyła; 1920-2005) was the 264th Pope of the Catholic Church, and one of the longest serving (26 years). He released the encyclical "On Human Work" in 1981; he was canonized in 2014.

Julian of Norwich (c. 1342-1416) was an anchoress – a recluse who lived in a cell attached to a church. Her visions occurred in 1373, when she was, as she and others thought, dying. Seeking for years after for an understanding of the visions, it was eventually shown to her that at their core the meaning was, simply and completely, love.

John Paul II. (2001). Apostolic Letter Novo Millennio Ineunte. https://www.vatican.va/content/john-paul-ii/en/apost_letters/2001/documents/hf_jp-ii_apl_20010106_novo-millennio-ineunte.html

Locklear, L. R., Taylor, S. G., & Ambrose, M. L. (2021). How a gratitude intervention influences workplace mistreatment: A multiple mediation model. *Journal of Applied Psychology*, *106*(9), 1314.

Maruta, T., Colligan, R. C., Malinchoc, M., & Offord, K. P. (2002, August). Optimism-pessimism assessed in the 1960s and self-reported health status 30 years later. In *Mayo Clinic Proceedings* (Vol. 77, No. 8, pp. 748-753). Elsevier.

Patil, M., Biswas, S., & Kaur, R. (2018). Does gratitude impact employee morale in the workplace. *Journal of Applied Management-Jidnyasa*, *10*(2), 21-36.

Seligman, M. E. (2006). *Learned optimism: How to change your mind and your life*. Vintage.

The Shewings of Julian of Norwich, Part 1. (1994). Georgia Ronan Crampton, Ed. https://d.lib.rochester.edu/teams/text/the-shewings-of-julian-of-norwich-part-1

Index